The concern of this book is to ask wl
roles of women in the church. It is an (
passages that matter, in the company of two compelling, qualified and
passionate guides. Elisabeth Goddard and Clare Hendry both love
and respect the Bible, both serve in significant roles of teaching and
scholarship, and both bring to this subject many years of personal study,
commitment and concern. But they don't agree on how these crucial
passages should be interpreted and applied. As I eavesdropped on their
conversation, I was struck by the pervasive gentleness of their discourse.
Here is a subject that for generations has engendered rage and rancour,
producing instead calm and considered prose. Neither writer moves
too far, in the end, from their starting position. But neither do they, along
the way, use words as weapons to destroy and denounce. I found this
valuable as a means by which to review and revisit the debate – and
refreshing as a lesson in how debate might be conducted. This book
demonstrates not only what women think and feel about ministry, but
how women tackle controversy. The irony was not lost on me, as a male
reader, and I wonder which other of our theological debates might
benefit if there were more women involved in debating them!
*Gerard Kelly, Co-Director, with his wife Chrissie, of the Bless Network
(www.blessnet.eu), and co-author, also with Chrissie, of* Intimate with the
Ultimate *(Authentic)*

Most treatments on the role of women in the church lob theological
hand grenades at a perceived enemy from an entrenched presupposition.
The Gender Agenda is something different, and so much the better for it.
Two women, both wives, mums, theologians and church pastors, differ
on exactly what ministry God calls and equips women to and share how
they have arrived at their interpretation of Scripture. Dialogue rather
than didactic, this mutual listening is a respectful, peaceful and robustly
biblical exchange. What is new here, and what makes this a valuable
contribution, is the manner in which the discussion is conducted, and
that very manner will help us better to listen and learn. This book may
not change your position, but it may change your attitude.
*Simon Ponsonby, Pastor of Theology, St Aldates, Oxford and Dean of Studies,
Oxford Centre for Church Growth*

This is an engaging book, theologically astute and earthed in real life and ministry. The lively emails helpfully reveal the nuances and subtleties of the evangelical debate surrounding women leaders in the church. *The Gender Agenda* offers a timely reminder not to judge but to listen, and demonstrates the power of holding strong Christian relationship whilst in profound disagreement.

Jackie Searle, Vicar of St Peter's, Littleover, and Dean of Women in the Derby Diocese

I warmly commend this book for the way in which it allows the reader to sit in on a healthy conversation between friends who find themselves in some areas of disagreement over the reading of the Bible. Retaining the friendly email format greatly assists the conversational tone, and helps us 'hear' them wrestling with the implications of their own thinking. Clare and Lis have given us insight into why they have come to their conclusions over the roles of men and women in ministry today. They have modelled careful attention to the biblical text and a willingness to really hear what each other has to say. They have also concluded the conversation with a greater awareness of where they are in disagreement, coupled with a desire to keep listening. The caricature of the Church of England at war over this issue is carefully dismantled by books such as *The Gender Agenda*. It shows us a helpful way to navigate through the complexities.

Revd Dr Simon Vibert, Wycliffe Hall Oxford

Lis Goddard & Clare Hendry

THE
GENDER
AGENDA

Discovering God's plan for church leadership

ivp

INTER-VARSITY PRESS
Norton Street, Nottingham NG7 3HR, England
Email: ivp@ivpbooks.com
Website: www.ivpbooks.com

First published 2010

British Library Cataloguing in Publication Data
A catalogue record for this book is available from the British Library

ISBN: 978-1-84474-494-7

Typeset by CRB Associates, Potterhanworth, Lincolnshire
Printed and bound in Great Britain by Ashford Colour Press Ltd, Gosport,
Hampshire

Contents

Acknowledgments

It seems a long time since the idea for this book came into being and we started writing the first chapter. Much has happened since then, both in our lives, as women serving God and juggling family life, and in the church. Needless to say, a few deadlines have passed, so first of all, many thanks for the incredible patience of our editors: to Sandra Byatt, who started out with us on this project; to Eleanor Trotter, who took it over as Sandra embarked on her own project – starting a family; and then to Kate Byrom, who has helped us see it through to completion. We have valued their support, encouragement and amazing editorial skills.

Lis: There are so many people I want to thank and need to thank. This book was written through some of the most difficult years of my life, and in many ways, it is a miracle of grace that it has seen the light of day at all. That grace manifested itself so often in the generous and overwhelming love of God's people who believed in me and loved me. I cannot thank everyone by name, but you know who you are and how important it was. However, I do need to mention our dear precious colleagues at Wycliffe Hall, who daily demonstrated for me what godly leadership looks like, even when things are really tough, and who loved us with the total self-giving love of God. Thank you too to those communities who loved us as the body of Christ: the student body at Wycliffe, St Andrew's North Oxford, Redland Parish Church and St Mary's Stoke Bishop.

These acknowledgments would not be complete, however, if I did not also thank my parents for teaching me that I was infinitely precious in God's eyes and had so much to offer. Thanks must go too to the OICCU Exec, on which Andrew and I met twenty-four years ago, for helping me / us to take that initial journey through the biblical text and to discover the wonder that lay there and the freedom of the new creation: they all remain precious friends and fellow travellers. Then there are the women of AWESOME, in particular the committee: it has been such a privilege to work with you, and I have learnt so much from you all. We do indeed serve an awesome God, and I am daily humbled that he has called me.

Clare: When I started out on what I thought would be my career, teaching RE in a secondary school, I had no idea that soon I would change direction, both in terms of the subject and the age of the students, and that I would later go on to be ordained, but God knew. He provided various people on the way to guide and encourage me in that journey. So thank you to Paul and Sharon Gardner, who were so influential in my change of direction and have been great friends ever since. Thank you also to Gordon Bridger, who bravely appointed me to the staff at Oak Hill College, and to Alex Ross, who was vicar at St James when I first joined the staff team. Gordon and Alex both modelled biblical male headship with such humility, and they have greatly encouraged me in my ministry. It was a privilege to work with them, as it was to work with colleagues at both Oak Hill and St James. Thank you to the many Christian sisters and friends who have shared cups of tea (and sometimes something stronger!), listened to me, prayed with me, cried and laughed with me and generally kept me sane during the time that I've been writing this book. In particular, Tamsin, Lynne, Diane and Laura, and also my recent prayer quadruplet, Gina, Jackie and Helen – you have all been stars! I am aware that, in naming specific people, I have missed out others who have been a great encouragement and support, so please consider yourselves appreciated and thanked too.

Lis: It is hard to know how to begin to thank my family for all the love and support they have given me through the writing of this book. They have been constant in their encouragement (and teasing) and steadfast in their love. When I have found the going hard because other things have been difficult, they have been consistently firm in their belief in me. I could not ask for more encouraging children or a more wonderful or faithful husband. Thank you for praying with me, thank you for loving me, thank you, each of you, for being you.

Clare: Finally, but by no means least, thanks to my family for their support and understanding during the writing of this book: to Kate and Alistair who seemed to cope with their mother being a little more distracted than usual; and to Steve who encouraged me in the first place to say yes to Lis.

Elisabeth Goddard
Clare Hendry
September 2010

For
Andrew, Jonathan and Nell
Steve, Kate and Alistair
with love and thanks

Foreword

Matters relating to gender have been part of the evangelical agenda for many centuries. Evangelical Christians, men as well as women, have been concerned to affirm that it is God who has made us male and female, and to explore the consequences of this in a myriad of roles and relationships that we experience: in the church, in family life and in society. There has always been the deep assumption that these things matter in the lived-out witness of the Christian life, through the observation of which people may come to know Christ as their Lord and Saviour. For many, the Bible is clear on these issues, and the answers to our current questions straightforward; for others, the biblical material has to be read differently from in the past. The questions we ask are commonly these: what roles and responsibilities are open to men and women in marriage and other family relationships? Should women lead and/or teach in the churches, and should women carry oversight responsibility in churches and in society? Through the last decades, one thing has become clearer now than in our past: women certainly have the gifts and abilities for leadership roles and responsibilities. We no longer argue for a particular view of gender roles and relationships based on a view of women as diminished or second-class human beings. Rather, we meet able, articulate and emotionally intelligent women in all kinds of settings in everyday life, often carrying significant levels of senior responsibility in their fields. What does this experience mean for evangelicals who want to use Scripture as the ground for understanding gender?

Recently I had a conversation with a woman who was beginning to sense a vocation to ordained ministry in the Church of England. Her home church was conservatively evangelical. It was a place where she had received a good grounding in the Christian faith, but it was not supportive of women in ordained ministry that involved leadership. This woman described how in this church for her to be able to begin to think through the issues involved, and to look again at what the Bible might be saying, she had had to separate emotionally and spiritually from her closest women friends. She spoke eloquently of the cost of this spiritual journey: it was difficult for these women to be together and to disagree. This separation for vocational discernment is unique to the evangelical constituency; it is not experienced to the same extent by women in any other part of the Church of England, and rarely by men at all. One mark of evangelicalism is that we separate too quickly when we disagree, finding it difficult to remain in dialogue, never mind relationship, when we find we hold to different opinions.

In *The Gender Agenda*, Lis Goddard and Clare Hendry take a look at some of the key questions relating to gender in the evangelical constituency of the Church of England today. Their method has as much to say to us as the biblical and theological material that they explore together. In writing this book, they have chosen to be in dialogue with each other in a way that is both personal and connected, as they describe their own life journeys, as well as the ongoing challenges as women coping with the usual demands of family relationships and friendships. Committed to relationship with each other beyond the task of writing this book, they know that they have much more in common as evangelicals and in their concern for the kingdom than that which might separate them when it comes to questions relating to gender. The exploration of familiar texts is rooted in their lives, which are full of the busyness of ministry, family and prayer. Their responses, sometimes converging, at other times diverging to differing conclusions, show that women evangelicals of whatever persuasion benefit from dialogues such as this, whether achieved in personal friendships or through wider support networks.

This book contains a model of theological discourse from which many – men as well as women – can learn.

Canon Anne Dyer
Warden of Cranmer Hall, Durham

Introduction

How do you write an accessible introductory book about whether women should be in leadership in the church? That was the question that I (Lis) was faced with after having been a reader for two excellent books (each arriving at clearly opposing conclusions) published by IVP on the subject, both of which required a fair amount of initial knowledge as a starting point. I loved them both, but felt concerned that there was nothing available for those just starting to grapple with these issues, and particularly, there seemed to be nothing that really engaged constructively with the opposing view, which you really need at the beginning of the process of discovery and discernment.

It occurred to me that the obvious solution would be a conversation between two women who had worked through the relevant texts and, having arrived at different conclusions, were willing to journey together and to take others with them. We came up with the idea of an email conversation, and decided to work through the biblical texts from Genesis to the Pastorals, batting our thoughts back and forth to help each other (and our readers, God willing) to see how we reached our different positions. When IVP asked me to write this book, I suggested that Clare should be my partner in crime. We had met and become good friends through AWESOME, a group for evangelical ordained women in the Church of England which I chair and on which Clare represents permanent deacons. At the time, we were both teaching at theological colleges and also serving on the staffs of large churches, so despite our very different understanding of the biblical teaching on women, we had a lot in common.

Clare: When Lis contacted me with this book proposal, I was somewhat daunted to say the least. But after prayer and encouragement from my husband, Steve, I said 'yes'. During my time on the staff of a theological college, I had been involved in various debates and discussions amongst evangelicals, on what women can and can't do in the church. Two things had frustrated me in those debates: the lack of real understanding, or sometimes even knowledge, of the opposite position; and the fact that a lot of time was spent debating the theological principles, but with much less emphasis on encouraging and training women to carry out their roles. This book seemed to be a way forward, a means of engaging with the different positions to see how they can begin to work out in practice within the church and leadership teams.

We have loved writing this book together and, although neither of us has radically changed our position, it is true to say that our friendship and trust have deepened, as has our love for God's Word. Our prayer is that it will be a source of blessing to you in your journey, as it has been to us.

1. Authoritative Women?
   Journeys of Discovery

From:	**Lis Goddard**
To:	Clare Hendry
Subject:	Making a start

Dear Clare

Perhaps it would be helpful for me to begin by telling you a bit about myself and how I got to where I am today – an evangelical woman ordained to the **priesthood** in the Church of England, and totally at ease with it under Scripture. As I look back, it seems remarkable that I ever got here – not because of the church, but because of my background.

I grew up in a **conservative**, evangelical Anglican church, where my father was the vicar and my mother, a strong and able woman, shared his ministry. My three brothers and I were always treated equally and encouraged to be all that we could be. There was never any distinction made between us in terms of education or expectations, and I was encouraged to use and develop all my gifts of leadership and pastoral care. However, it was always made absolutely clear that, if we read Scripture honestly and take it seriously, then women shouldn't be ordained; women are not called or allowed to lead in the church.

This wasn't an oppressive or a destructive knowledge. It was rather like saying that you knew that women were the ones who had children and men were the ones who shaved their beards. I just accepted it as a fact of life within a world in which I was genuinely loved and nurtured. I don't know that I ever had any overwhelming desire to change the system or to prove it wrong. All I ever really wanted was to serve my Lord whom I loved with all my heart, and I knew I would do that, whatever it meant.

At eighteen I got a place at Oxford to read theology, which was really exciting. I don't think that I ever enjoyed anything quite as much as struggling with my faith, and finding it becoming more and more alive, and deeper and richer as I worked at it.

While I was at Oxford I was asked to serve on the OICCU (Oxford Inter-Collegiate Christian Union) Executive Committee as one of the vice-presidents (which is how I met Andrew whom I later married). Our committee arrived with a mandate from the membership to review the constitution. This stated that all OICCU presidents should be men, and that there should at all times be a majority of men on the committee. We spent much of the following year struggling with the biblical passages that referred to the calling of men and women, putting them in the context of the scriptural witness as a whole, reading every book we could find on the subject, writing papers for one another and praying, praying, praying. It was a hard and painful year.

To the surprise of some of us, by the end of the year we had changed the constitution, and I had changed my mind. I had become absolutely convinced that the traditional understanding of the biblical texts, while possible, made no sense within the whole teaching of Scripture.

Alongside all of this, I still had a sense that I wanted to serve God in some way, but didn't know how. I didn't think I wanted to be a vicar. I had grown up in a vicarage and I didn't want that for my family. It is a hard calling and I didn't think I could do it.

I went to work as research assistant for Tom Wright while he was Chaplain of Worcester College in Oxford. He had been one of my tutors and I had really enjoyed working with him. When the Assistant Chaplain left and he was unable to get an ordained replacement, he asked whether I could fill in for him in a lay capacity. I agreed, thinking that it would only be for a few weeks. I did it for nearly two years! After just two weeks of sharing in the pastoral work, I remember saying to Andrew, 'I have found the shape God cut me in.' I couldn't do anything else – I just had to be ordained! The time finally came to train for the ministry, and Andrew and I decided to train together. We felt strongly called to job-share so that we could also job-share the parenting of our two, then very small, children, Jonathan and Nell.

My father was still very involved in the General Synod and was a leading figure in the **evangelical** movement to prevent the **ordination** of women to the priesthood. How was I to tell him about my decision? It was really hard – he was convinced that if I were to be ordained I would be going against Scripture, and so we spent a lot of time talking together, reading the Bible, praying and crying together. In the end, it became absolutely clear that neither of us was going to persuade the other. We reached the point where we were able to say that, although we disagreed, we knew that the other was under Scripture and that we trusted each other – and this was the most significant thing we could do.

When I came to be ordained as a priest, my father didn't lay hands on me, but beforehand he promised that he would pray for me and my ministry every day of his life, and that is so much more valuable.

That is why I want to write this book with you, Clare, because I want to help others who disagree as profoundly as we do, or as I do with my father, nevertheless to be able to work together for **the kingdom**. I still think that I am right in my understanding of the biblical teaching, which has profound implications for male–female relations and for how we lead our churches. Otherwise, I couldn't continue in ordained ministry with integrity, but I want to be able to work alongside other labourers in the harvest field.

Having read that long screed, I wonder whether you would still like to embark on this enterprise with me.

With best wishes in Christ
Lis

From:	**Clare Hendry**
To:	Lis Goddard
Subject:	Picking up the baton

Hi Lis

After speaking to you on the phone I was really excited by this project, but equally totally daunted. Time was a big factor. After working at Oak Hill Theological College for nearly nineteen years in various capacities, I have decided that I should cut down my working hours. I felt it was right now to concentrate more on my family and on ministry at St James's (my local church), and to juggle fewer things.

After your call I discussed the book with Steve (my husband). He strongly encouraged me to go for it if I really wanted to. So despite all my apprehensions about time, ability, etc., what finally persuaded me were the sentiments that you expressed towards the end of your email. Like you, I am keen to see how we, as two women holding a different position on women's ministry, can debate in a way that will help us engage with the texts, look at how we live them out in our different lives and, above all, how we can still enjoy Christian fellowship and encourage each other as we seek to serve God faithfully.

Over the years I have thought a lot about women in ministry. Unlike you, I wasn't brought up in a Christian home, but came to faith through my school Christian Union. At university I attended an Anglican evangelical church, which became more **charismatic** during my time there. I wasn't aware of any particular position regarding women's ministry being taught there. I spent some time in Cambridge doing a post-graduate certificate of education, and then teaching RE for a couple of years.

While doing a bit of sorting out recently (a rare thing in the Hendry household!), I came across an essay I wrote back in the eighties at Reformed Theological Seminary in the States. I spent two years there doing a Masters in 'Marriage and Family Therapy'. About half the course concentrated on biblical and theological subjects, and the rest was on counselling. It was the first time I had ever seriously studied the Bible. I had to write an essay on 'Male and Female in Paul's Theology', and I think this was when I first began to grapple with what the Bible teaches about men and women.

At that time, while I felt called to work in the area of counselling and (for some strange reason) to work in the Church of England, I wasn't particularly thinking about ordination. However, as time went by and the course was reaching its end, I realized that the best way of fulfilling that call practically was to go for ordination. On returning to the UK in the mid-eighties, I went on a **selection conference**. However, God closed that door and I wasn't recommended. I ended up being an administrator at a psychiatric hospital in Cambridge (which was good training for what followed) and I was involved in counselling at my local church.

I still felt called to counselling and to the Church of England, but wasn't sure how to pursue that, when I heard about a full-time post as Lecturer in Pastoral Counselling at Oak Hill College. I had barely heard of Oak Hill and wasn't really sure what I might be letting myself in for, but to cut a long story short, I was offered the post, and began teaching there in 1986. On the way, I picked up a husband, two children and a **dog collar**.

Oak Hill has certainly been an interesting place to work, and on the whole I have loved my time there. The debate on women's ministry has been an ongoing one. At times I guess I have been seen as very conservative, but equally I have had a couple of students walk out of chapel when I was preaching – in preaching to a mixed congregation I was obviously not conservative enough for them.

When I decided that God might be calling me to pursue ordination again, I felt fairly clear that I should go for the permanent **diaconate** (i.e. not become a priest). My diocese was not the easiest place for a woman who wanted to be priested, but that wasn't my reason for choosing that path. I was still not convinced that it was right for a woman to be a vicar. While I wholeheartedly believe in the 'priesthood of all believers' (1 Peter 2:9), I was unsure about the implications of being priested, particularly if one saw it as a **presbyter**'s or elder's role with the implication of authority.

So here I am – a Minister of Pastoral Care at St James Muswell Hill, and a visiting lecturer at Wycliffe Hall, Oxford; still a **deacon** and still wondering if at some stage I might go forward to the priesthood.

This is a long-winded way of saying that I am very willing to join you in trying to write this book! As we both have heavy work and family commitments, email seems like the best way to debate.

As well as showing how women can debate and disagree, and yet still work together, I think it would be great if this book could also show the variety within the two different groups that we represent – namely those who endorse female vicars and those who don't. Both parties have been guilty of caricaturing the other side, and do not always understand that even within the two groups there are different ways in which each position is held.

Look forward to hearing from you
Best wishes
Clare

From:	**Lis Goddard**
To:	Clare Hendry
Subject:	Under starter's orders

Dear Clare
It was a relief to receive such an honest answer from you. I sometimes feel as though I am the only one juggling twenty impossible things before breakfast! I am sure that we will struggle to find time to write, and family crises are bound to cause deadlines to slip, but I am totally convinced that this is worth striving for.

If anything really frustrates me about this whole debate, it is how the different sides tend to fire off books *at* one another rather than listening *to* one another. If we can model something different, then that has to be of value in the grand scheme of things – even if it's only a drop in the ocean. It is incredibly frustrating when it is assumed that you can be trusted only if you take a certain view, so if our conversation / emails can help to dispel that, then so much the better.

Having spent several years working with students and young people (among others), I know how very important this whole issue is for them – not that we tell them what to believe, but that we go some way to providing the tools to begin to think through the issues, as these are some of the questions that students and many ordinary Christians are always asking.

This is also a hot topic for many within our own denomination (Church of England) at the moment, and will continue to be so for several years to come, as we debate the whole question of women bishops. Many lay men and women will be asking the fundamental question about whether or not women could or should have authority in the church as ultimately held within Anglicanism by bishops. Our society constantly poses the question to the church, so we have to be ready with a carefully thought-out answer – an answer determined not by the pressures of political correctness, but by prayer and careful theological reflection on God's Word.

Like you, I hope that we will be able to challenge some pre-conceived ideas and our **core constituencies**, but I also hope that we will be able to challenge ourselves, because if we are not challenged we will not grow.

I am very excited about working through the biblical texts again with you and having you take me to task. Where do you want to start? Genesis?

All the best
Lis

To ponder

What have been the major influences on your journey as you have explored the role of women in the church?

Which women have influenced you in your spiritual life?

Pray

Spend some time thanking God for those who have nurtured you. Ask God to be your guide as you journey though his Word and seek to gain understanding.

2. Let's start at the very beginning: Creation

Suggested reading: Genesis 1 – 3

From:	**Clare Hendry**
To:	Lis Goddard
Subject:	Let's start at the very beginning

Dear Lis

Now to business!

I never had much of a handle on the Old Testament until I did a wonderful course at the seminary, 'Old Testament Introduction' with Dr VanGemeren. It particularly gave me a love for the opening chapters of Genesis.

I regard Genesis 1 – 3 as the most fundamental chapters on man and woman in the Old Testament, and from which everything else follows, in both the Old and New Testaments. What is clear, as I am sure you agree, is that God created both men and women in his image, and that together they represent God. We see this right back in Genesis 1:27–28 – man and woman together making up the human species:

So God created man
    in his own image,
in the image of God
    he created him;
male and female
    he created them.

> God blessed them and said to them, 'Be fruitful and increase in number; fill the earth and subdue it. Rule over the fish of the sea and the birds of the air and over every living creature that moves on the ground.'

There is a sense of equality and worth, which we see reflected again in Genesis 2:18–25.

'Equality', however, does not mean 'the same'. Men and women are different. We can see that in the different ways in which they are created: Adam from the dust and Eve from Adam, and they are given different names and roles. So there is a distinction right from creation that is reflected in the roles to which men and women are called: Adam is commanded to work and take care of the garden; Eve is to be a helper (Genesis 2:15–18). There is a sense that they are complementary to each other, which is why I am all in favour of mixed-gender teams in ministry. The *order* in which Adam and Eve are created also has significance, with Adam first and Eve following. As I understand it, Adam's headship was established before **the Fall** and is not a result of the Fall. These distinctions are reflected in later passages in Scripture in the New Testament.

When Adam is given the task of naming the animals – part of his job of exercising dominion and reflecting his authority over them – he is unable to find a companion for himself. God declares that it is not good for man to be alone. So God creates an appropriate companion for him. The **Hebrew** word for 'helper' suggests one who will play a subordinate role in some sense. It does not necessarily indicate inferiority. After all, it is used of God when he helps human leaders, e.g. in Exodus 18:4. But when this word is used in the Old Testament, it seems that the context is always that of a person helping someone who is carrying the primary responsibility for whatever is going on. I think this sets the pattern for the relationship between man and woman, and certainly does not make the woman inferior in any way.

I realize that I have made various statements here without unpacking how I arrived at them. I would love to hear your take on them.

Hope your term is going well. Look forward to hearing from you soon.

Love
Clare

From:	**Lis Goddard**
To:	Clare Hendry
Subject:	Image quality

Dear Clare

Sorry to have taken some time to reply: Jonathan has been puzzling over his A level options and Nell over her GCSE options. It is very exciting to watch them thinking about their future and considering where God might be calling them. I love the fact that they can both ask those questions freely, not just Jonathan. It would be really sad if Nell felt that she couldn't or shouldn't be expecting to be used by God in leadership roles in whatever sphere he calls her to. And I guess that is what this book is about – what is it that God created us, men and women, for?

Your introduction to Genesis gave a good overview of the issues. I will take the points you make one at a time and in detail, and bat them back to you.

I find the language in Genesis 1:27ff. fascinating. Here the Hebrew word 'ādām is used to refer to both the man and the woman (indeed, it doesn't take a pronoun and thus become a proper name until after the Fall). It is generic rather than specific, referring to humanity in general:

So God created human beings
   in his own image,
in the image of God he created them;
   male and female he created them.
(Genesis 1:27)

I know that you deduce equality from this passage too. However, I am not sure how you define it, given that you go on to read things into the text which I am not at all sure are there. I agree entirely that men and women are different, but I am not sure that Genesis 1 – 3 indicates a distinction reflected in their different roles.

Immediately after these verses comes the clear implication of this imaging: male and female both receive God's blessing and jointly are recipients of his commands to be fruitful and multiply, and to fill the earth and subdue it. They are both to rule over the earth. In other words, they are both recipients of what it is to be made in the image of God – to be in relationship, to be caught up in the creative dynamic, and to be entrusted with dominion. There is no hint here that the dominant 'role' of ruler is to be the man's: at this stage it is to be held and exercised jointly as they image God in his world. Here surely we see true equality and relationship as God intended it to be and, as we move on to the **narrative** in chapters 2 and 3, we will see how this goes wrong as the Fall throws everything out of kilter.

Anyway, I am going to leave it there so that you can come back to me on what I have written and perhaps move us on to the next bit of the story.

With love in Christ
Lis

From:	**Clare Hendry**
To:	Lis Goddard
Subject:	Role play

Dear Lis
It's my turn to apologize for taking so long to get back to you. The last few weeks have been a bit manic. You'd think I would learn to say no to things after so many years in ministry, but that's a lesson I'm still learning!

I hope life at your end is calming down a bit. Kate is in the middle of GCSEs, so A level options are looming. We have just heard that Alistair has got a place at Owens, where Kate goes, so he will be heading off there next September. I quite understand how you feel about wanting to see Jonathan and Nell reach the potential for which God has created them, including being used in any leadership roles God may call them to. This book has particular relevance for our daughters.

In many areas of life, such as politics or business, I think that overall leadership is open to both men and women alike. However, I do believe that within the areas of church and family God has laid down distinct roles, where there is a pattern of male headship or leadership, but which doesn't preclude women from some shared form of leadership. Indeed, I would want to argue strongly that leadership teams in churches should be mixed. My reasons for taking such a view will become clearer as we look at the biblical passages.

Thanks for your response to my initial comments. I'd be interested to hear more specifically about what you felt I had read into the passage. I do agree that it might be difficult to see how some of my observations on Genesis come directly from the actual text. But the comments are made in the light of other passages as, I am sure you would agree, 'Scripture must interpret Scripture'. Inevitably I read passages in the Old Testament in the light of the New Testament.

I am not convinced that there is no distinction between the roles of Adam and Eve before the Fall. I have always understood the Genesis 1 account to be rather an overview, looking at how God created humankind and what they were to do, i.e. created in the image of God (male and female) and then to be fruitful and rule over the earth (Genesis 1:28). Genesis 2 (before the Fall) seems to look in greater depth at how male and female were to work together in fulfilling God's commands. How do you understand that in this account Adam was created first and, having no suitable companion, Eve was then created to be his helper and fulfil this role?

Certainly the Fall threw things out of kilter, but not perhaps in the way you suggest. I see the relationship between Adam and Eve clearly affected by the Fall in terms of the way they work together. Instead of the harmony that God created between them, we now have men dominating in a heavy-handed way rather than exercising a godly headship (akin to being a team leader), and women fighting against this headship. Interestingly, in marriage counselling situations I also see a slightly different pattern, where the wife seems to assume headship because her husband has opted out. The principles established by God before the Fall – man and woman created in the image of God, to fill the earth and rule over it together – still exist after the Fall, as do the implications of Adam being created first, and then Eve.

Where headship is exercised in a biblical way, it can be liberating. I see Steve as head of our family. Steve and I certainly do not have a perfect marriage, and so sometimes the way we relate to each other is more a reflection of our sinfulness than of the roles that I believe God has ordained for us. But the more we actually work together in the way we are called to, and the less self-centred we are, the better things are. The way Steve exercises headship is by no means dominating; rather, he tries to lead in a way that puts God at the centre of family life and that will help build up each family member. We will look at this later when we come to such passages as Ephesians 5.

I would love to hear more from you on Genesis 2 and how you understand the order of creation. It would be helpful too to hear why you think God cursed Adam and Eve in different ways if there are no real differences between them with respect to roles.

Back now to planning one of our Good Friday meditation slots. As we debate back and forth, it's great to be reminded that the most important thing we share is the good news of Easter and all that that means.

Look forward to hearing back from you soon. Hope you have a great Easter.

Love
Clare

From:	**Lis Goddard**
To:	Clare Hendry
Subject:	As God is my helper

Dear Clare

Things have been complicated here with a change of job and a house move. It has been a strange time, and I have found myself caught up in doing all sorts of things that I never imagined I would do – such as home-schooling Nell for a month while we looked for a new school for her – quite an experience for both of us! Actually it was a privilege to spend so much extra time with her at such a key point in her education. Now here we are happily settled in Bristol, and I can once again give my mind to Genesis.

Thank you for your careful response to my last email. You are of course right that the key place we will differ will be Genesis 1 – 3. Although we generally agree with each other on Genesis 1:26–28, where we disagree there lays the foundation for all that follows. I still want to see the great opening **commission** and calling of Genesis 1:26ff. as God's welcome and commissioning of all humanity, irrespective of gender. I do not see any hint here of differentiation or hierarchy. In fact, I would suggest that its very wording excludes this. Both male and female are to have dominion over creation, and this surely precludes either one exercising dominion over the other. I wonder whether the temptation to suggest otherwise comes from reading back into it certain understandings taken (I think wrongly) from the following chapters, and indeed from other passages of Scripture. Like you, I believe that 'Scripture must interpret Scripture', but we must be careful that that is indeed what is happening, and not our own interpretation in the light of cultural biases – I speak to myself here too.

I understand Genesis 1 – 3 to be fundamental for a good and clear understanding of the relationship between men and women and their calling under God in the world. We have to be very careful not to get into a circular argument which does not allow this key foundational passage to challenge our thinking because we believe we already know what it says.

When writing about the Genesis 2 story, you said that it looks at 'how male and female were to work together in fulfilling God's commands'. Here you particularly build on the fact that Adam was created first. Clearly this is indisputable from the narrative, but the conclusions I want to draw from that are very different from yours. Order in creation does not imply hierarchy or authority to me; nowhere do I find this stated in the text – except perhaps in the fact that the man has dominion and authority over the animals. I don't think that we can have it both ways: man is created *after* the animals, etc., and so he is given authority over them; he is created *before* the woman and so he is given authority over her. It doesn't make sense logically, quite apart from not being there in the Bible text. I would not want to deduce from this that the woman, as the final one to be created, has the ultimate power and authority, although I know that some have said that.

On the contrary, I do not believe this narrative has anything to do with power or authority, or roles in male/female relationships. Indeed, when we start thinking in those terms, we are missing the point and talking in post-Fall language. I am sure that this passage has much more to do with how we image God, how we are in relationship with one another, and how that looks at its best.

It is key that it is God who recognizes that 'It is not good for the man to be alone' (Genesis 2:18). Quite apart from anything else, it is remarkable after Genesis 1, where God has looked at his creation and has consistently seen that 'it was good', for him now to look at something and say 'It is not good.' This is the Genesis 2 equivalent of Genesis 1:27, which uses the singular and then the plural to express that humanity as a whole are in the image of God, but that that image is expressed in community ('male and female he created them'). God, who expresses the most fundamental part of his being through relationship in the **Trinity**, here recognizes that if man is to be truly in his image he must not be alone. Man (humanity) must be in community. The man must be in an inter-dependent, self-giving, loving relationship with another. Otherwise the image becomes a mere parody, not even approaching the multi-faceted dimensions of the original.

It is hardly surprising then that no helper is found for the man from among the animals: remember that God promises 'a helper suitable for him'. Neither is it surprising that the man's response to the woman is one of delight and recognition. He sees her and knows her to be the same as him: 'This is now bone of my bones and flesh of my flesh' (Genesis 2:23). Even his acknowledgment of her otherness reflects their unity: 'she shall be called "woman", for she was taken out of man' (Genesis 2:23). This is not the man naming the woman – a different verb is used here, and Adam's naming of Eve significantly comes after the Fall (Genesis 3:20). This is much more: it is Adam's recognition of himself in her. In Hebrew the word for 'woman' ('iššâ) sounds very like that for 'man' ('ish).

Here is the helper promised by God – a helper so like him as to be part of him and to match him. As you rightly say, the term 'helper' is often used throughout the Old Testament, including of God in his relation to humankind. Indeed, it is used more often in relation to God than to anyone else. It is hard then to see how one can say that 'in the Old Testament the context is always that of a person helping someone else, who is carrying the primary respon-sibility for whatever is going on'. As I understand it, in all our dealings with God he is always the lead partner. We are engaged in his work, however inadequately, and ultimately the responsibility is his. You suggest that, when we or the Old Testament speak of God being our helper, we are in some way casting him as 'one who will play a subordinate role in some sense'. This sounds dangerous. Are we claiming this mainly because we want or need to assert something about the respective roles of men and women? I find it very difficult to see how you can conclude a subordinate role for women from the language of 'helper', given that you acknowledge that the term is used of God.

Please don't misunderstand me, I am very clear that men and women are different. Otherwise, when the man first saw the woman, he would have recognized the other as *'îš* rather than *'iššâ*. However, I do not believe that this passage gives us a warrant for suggesting that this difference is based on their God-given *roles*. I just do not find it here.

Well, I haven't even touched on the Fall and its implications for our relationships. But I am guessing that you will want to respond to these points first.

I do hope that you are all well. I am guessing that Kate must be doing, or have just done, her GCSE mocks – has she coped all right? We had GCSEs in the summer and we are now in the middle of AS levels. Jonathan has just taken exams in four modules after just one term's teaching, which seems like barely enough time to assimilate the knowledge. Things were so different in my day!

With much love in Christ
Lis

From:	**Clare Hendry**
To:	Lis Goddard
Subject:	Order and disorder

Dear Lis
It's great to hear that you are settling down to life in Bristol. I hope Nell and Jonathan are happy at their new schools and making good friends. We had Alistair's first parents' evening at his new school. Life seems to be moving so quickly – he is already halfway through his first year. Kate had mocks just after Christmas, and GCSEs loom ahead.

We could have done with this book a few months ago. We had a discussion in the PCC (Parochial Church Council) on women in ministry. We were trying to provide the members with good, accessible material to help them to look at the issues from both sides. It was difficult to find any that didn't demand a theology degree and a month to read! We wanted to decide who to interview to join the clergy team. We did actually appoint a man, but that was certainly not a reflection of the outcome of the debate. He just happened to be the best candidate for the position. We also inter-viewed two very able women, who could well have been appointed if any other positions had been available.

Thank you for your very thoughtful reply to my last email. Again, you said so much that I wholeheartedly agree with, but I don't see how you arrived at some of your conclusions, or at least I can see how you got there, but don't agree with how you got there.

I am right with you on Genesis 1 as 'God's welcome and commissioning of all humanity irrespective of gender'. Adam and Eve are called to have dominion over the rest of creation. I agree that there is no hint of hierarchy in this chapter, but surely that doesn't mean that it isn't present elsewhere in Scripture. Genesis 1 cannot contain comprehensively all that is foundational for what comes later.

With regard to your comments on my arguments from creation order, I see what you are saying on the logic and, if we argue directly from the order of creation, animals would be supreme, but that was not my intention. It is clear that God's relationship with his creation up to the creation of humankind was different from his relationship with man and woman. As we read through Genesis 1, we see that God said, '*Let there be* light' (verse 3), '*Let there be* an expanse between the waters . . .* ' (verse 6), '*Let the* water . . .* ' (verse 9), and so on, but when creating humankind the formula changes to '*Let us make* man in our image' (verse 26).

In all of the acts of creation up to the creation of humankind, God's words were a **formula of fiat**, but when God came to create humankind he used a **formula of counsel**. So God's relationship with humankind and his relationship with the rest of creation were clearly different. The rest of creation was not meant to be in his image. So I am only arguing from the order of creation of humankind, as distinct from the rest of creation. I realize that you draw different conclusions. At one level I think you are right, as it does not explicitly say in the text that man is the head over woman. However, from references to Genesis in other parts of Scripture, it can be argued that Adam is head over Eve, so I think that we will need to come back to this later when we look at Ephesians 5.

Let me now move on to what you were saying about 'It is not good for the man to be alone.' I love the way that you stress the importance of community. It is so clear that we were never created to live without significant relationships, whether they be husband and wife, child and parent or friend and friend. When I was teaching a pastoral counselling course at a theological college, we started by looking at the biblical view of personhood and considering some of the implications of being created in the image of God. One of the things I highlighted was this need to be in relationship with one another. It is such a fundamental part of who we are and how God created us to be. I think you are right to highlight the Trinity as the way God is in relationship, which we need to reflect as his image-bearers.

Regarding the concept of helper, I realize that I raised some issues without going into any depth. You are absolutely right to say that if we are not careful we could cast God in some subordinate role, which is clearly unbiblical, and I agree that the term 'helper' does suggest subordination. I realize that it is a term occasionally used of God in the Old Testament. Clearly God cannot be subordinate to humankind, but I do think that God can subordinate himself to humankind in some sense. Surely he does that in a way by helping us according to his sovereign, gracious will. We could also talk about Jesus subordinating himself and serving us by being willing to die in our place on the cross; yet we would certainly not say he became less divine in any way.

Having said all of that, in Genesis 2 the woman's role is portrayed as different from the man's, and is best encapsulated in the term 'helper'. As I reread Genesis 2 and looked at various commentaries, I still couldn't see how to reconcile the facts in Genesis 2:7. Adam was created first, God took him and put him in the garden of Eden to work it and take care of it, and finally in verses 16–17 God commanded him not to eat of the tree of the knowledge of good and evil: all of this took place before the woman was created. So there are surely implications here for the way in which Adam and Eve relate to each other and carry out God's will for humankind.

That is probably enough from me. At some stage we may have to agree to disagree. There is so much more to explore. It would be great to hear a few responses to what I have said, and then maybe you can go on to look at how you understand Genesis 3 and the impact of the Fall on humankind.

Look forward to hearing back from you.
Clare

From:	**Lis Goddard**
To:	Clare Hendry
Subject:	Hide and seek

Dear Clare

How good to hear from you so quickly – we are becoming remarkably efficient!

It sounds as if your household like mine is mired in exams – it is now Nell's turn and she has just had her first three GCSE papers. Once more she hardly seems to have started the courses and here she is sitting the exams!

Although there are many points on which we agree, we are also really beginning to show up the cracks between us. The big one which I suspect we shall come across again and again seems to be how we apply Scripture – surprise, surprise! We both agree absolutely that Scripture is authoritative, but how that works out in practice is the deal-breaker.

For me, the fact that Genesis 2 does not speak of a relationship of dominance between the man and the woman, or of one being the 'head', is important in how we are to interpret it. I do not want to read in something that is not there, and its absence tells me something about creation, the nature of the Fall and indeed about what we find in other parts of the Bible. I quite agree that Scripture must interpret Scripture, but I suspect that we will disagree on what the rest of Scripture actually means, particularly Paul's letters. So it is really important to get a clear understanding of these passages in Genesis. I think we fundamentally disagree about the meaning of 'head' and how that then plays out as an interpreter of other parts of Scripture.

I am also not entirely sure that your position is consistent. In an earlier email, you said that in many areas of life overall leadership is open to both men and women alike, but that God has laid down a distinct pattern of roles within the church and the family. If your understanding of those roles in Genesis is based on creation order, as you say, then I do not see how women can be permitted to take on any work or leadership roles which are strictly speaking 'men's'. In Genesis there is no distinction between church work and secular work, and therefore if one is to be consistent, one would have to forbid women from doing anything that was man's domain prior to her creation. However, I would want to argue that being a helper means sharing equally in these tasks.

I also still have real problems with your equation of subordination and the language of helper, not least because I am not at all sure that one should ever say of God that he 'can subordinate himself to humanity': give himself in love for – yes, but subordinate himself to – no. To subordinate means to submit to a higher authority, and that surely cannot be right.

I must now move on to look at the Fall. For me this is the crux of when the relationship between man and woman changed, when things moved from that **mutuality** intended by God to the dominance of the curse.

The temptation first. Why the woman was tempted is an interesting question and clearly one which we cannot answer. Was it because she was the weaker partner? The man has obviously shared God's commands with the woman, as you would expect him to do with his helper with whom he shared everything. From the narrative there can therefore be no doubt that they are both guilty. Had the snake approached the man, we would always have asked whether the judgment was fair on the woman. Did she know? Was she given a choice? This way it is clear: they both knew and both chose – as shown in the telling phrase, 'her husband, who was with her' (Genesis 3:6).

It is significant here that the snake is clearly usurping *God's authority* over Eve; his attack is never represented as against the man's authority. 'You will not certainly die . . . For God knows that when you eat of it your eyes will be opened, and you will be like God, knowing good and evil' (3:4–5). Thus, when Eve decides to eat, it is this – the right hierarchy between humanity and God – that she and the man (when he then also decides to eat) are undermining, rather than any supposed natural hierarchy between the man and the woman.

After they have eaten of the forbidden fruit, the immediate result is the destruction of relationship. The man and the woman cover themselves and go from a place of total ease where the man is naturally 'with her' (3:6) to a feeling of self-consciousness in each other's company. They also hide from God for whom they were created. This surely tells us above all else what is at the heart of both the creation and the Fall. The freedom of relationship is now broken, which is summed up in the judgments that God utters in response to their disobedience. He curses both the earth and the snake, and then proceeds to pass judgment on the man and the woman. Interesting here is both the order and the content of these judgments.

It has been suggested that God speaks first to the man as a sign of his position of authority. In fact, this is never stated in the text, and it makes much more sense as a reflection of the fact that Adam was given the command and therefore should have been responsible. If I tell my daughter that I do not want a particular packet of biscuits to be eaten, asking her to pass on my injunction to my son, and then come home to find that the biscuits have gone, I will naturally first ask her what went wrong before moving on to my son. This is what God does here. He asks the man what has happened before moving on to the woman, which gives each of them the chance to explain and to demonstrate amply the full destructive horror of what has occurred. Adam: 'The woman *you* put here with me – *she* gave me some fruit from the tree, and I ate it.' Eve: 'The *snake* deceived me, and I ate' (my italics). Where previously there was harmony, recognition and unity between God and humanity, man and woman, and humanity and beast, now there is only accusation and enmity. God's response reflects this. He hears their recriminations and addresses each of the protagonists, beginning with the snake.

Here we also see the first judgment – the judgment of enmity between the snake and the woman's offspring. This demonstrates something important about the judgments generally: they have the character of confirmation. In his judgment God confirms what has inevitably happened as a result of the Fall. Because the woman listened to the snake, there is already enmity between them: see her accusatory response to God's question. The same is true of the key judgment of the woman and the man. To use the language of Romans 1, God hands them over to their newly discovered sinful desires. 'They exchanged the truth of God for a lie' (Romans 1:25), and 'Although they claimed to be wise, they became fools and exchanged the glory of the immortal God for images . . . ' (Romans 1:22–23). Thus when God says to the woman, 'Your desire will be for your husband and he will rule over you' (Genesis 3:16), he is confirming what has already happened: they have exchanged the full beauty of what it means to be made in the image of God for a pale imitation.

Their relationship of harmony and unity has been destroyed and is now characterized by dominance and strife. This is the first time in the text of Genesis that the language of ruling is used to refer to the relationship between the man and the woman. It is striking that it follows the Fall and the destruction of easy unity, mutual knowledge and recognition. What is interesting too is its use alongside the language of desire. This has often been interpreted to mean sexual desire, which is odd since sexual desire was clearly part of the pre-Fall, 'one-flesh' harmony. Given that exactly the same words are also used together in Genesis 4:7, where God says to Cain, 'sin is crouching at your door; it desires to have you, but you must rule over it', it is more likely to mean that there will now be a desire to dominate on the part of the woman. In other words, instead of the self-giving, mutual love of the Trinity for which they were created, we now have a struggle of wills between the man and the woman.

Immediately we begin to see the outworking of this, as the first thing the man does after God has spoken is to name the woman. Before the Fall he greeted her with recognition and joy as part of himself and intrinsically different from the animals, but now he establishes his authority by naming her.

It is interesting that we do not take it as binding for all time that all men must be farmers, and yet there seems to be the assumption that the judgment that impacts our relationships cannot be redeemed.

I look forward to hearing back from you, and then I guess we should move on to look at women in the rest of the Bible – if I can tear myself away from Genesis . . .

With love in Christ
Lis

From:	**Clare Hendry**
To:	Lis Goddard
Subject:	Rise and fall

Dear Lis
I hope Nell's exams went well. Steve and I are busy trying to convince Kate that a little bit of revision could be a good thing – not sure we have succeeded yet! I am just so glad that I don't have to do any more exams!

Thanks for your latest email. I am totally with you on the importance of Genesis for our debate. While it definitely lays the foundation for what is to follow, we can't just examine it in isolation from the rest of Scripture. So I am sure that, as we go on to look at what else the Bible has to say about women and their role, we will continue to refer back to Genesis.

It's interesting that you use the word 'dominance' when respond-ing to what I said about Genesis 2 and the relationship between man and woman. Nowadays 'dominance' seems to carry with it the concept of lording over someone – a far cry from what I think Scripture teaches about the relationship between a man and a woman. You then go on to look at my distinction between the roles of women in the church and family as compared to the secular world. I quite understand why you would regard it as inconsistent, but, in looking at Scripture, I see male headship being applied only to the areas of family and church life. Elsewhere there are examples, for instance Proverbs 31, where women take a position of headship in other areas, such as business. In working out the roles that God has set for men and women back in Genesis, they are seen as being fulfilled only within the realms of church and family. No doubt we will be looking at some examples in our later emails.

With regard to your comment on my equation of subordination and the language of helper, I think my reasoning will become clearer when we look at the Trinity in chapter 6.

Much of what you were saying about Genesis resonates with what I was teaching on biblical personhood at Oak Hill in my 'Introduction to Pastoral Care and Counselling' module. And I can say 'Amen' to what you say about the Fall. But again we diverge on the understanding of the consequences of the Fall. Obviously since you do not see headship as being present before the Fall, it must be seen as a consequence of it.

But I think it can be equally argued, as indeed many biblical scholars do, that the effects of the Fall reflect the presence of headship before the Fall. I will try briefly to explain my reading of the Fall.

The serpent has engaged Eve in conversation, twisting what God has said and distorting the commands that God had given to Adam, for instance, lessening the punishment from certain death: – 'will surely die' (Genesis 2:17) to 'lest you die' (Genesis 3:3 ESV), a sort of 'in case you die'. The serpent goes on to question even that: 'You will not surely die' (Genesis 3:4).

Eve took the lead from Adam as she was deceived by the serpent and led the way into sin. What was Adam doing meanwhile? Well, it seems that he was standing by and yet doing nothing to stop Eve from taking the fruit. Adam forsook his responsibility, his headship. Both were wrong, and through them sin and death entered the human race. It was role reversal that led to the Fall.

If you hold the view that Adam's sin included abandoning the responsibility of headship, as I do, it is significant that God calls out to Adam first. After all, in Romans 5:12–21 why does Paul blame only Adam for the Fall if both Adam and Eve were joint rulers/heads?

So what were the consequences of the Fall? Eve was to suffer in childbirth (Genesis 3:16). As mothers, Lis, you and I can certainly testify to that reality! Eve was to suffer in relation to her husband. Because she took over the headship in the temptation, God gives her over to the misery of competition with her rightful head. The second part of verse 16 is unclear. It could be that she will suffer conflict with her husband, and we can certainly see much evidence of that around us. Or it could mean that she will suffer domination by him. In other words, headship will be exercised not in the loving way that God established before the Fall, but in a domineering and ungodly way.

Adam had sinned by defying God's command not to eat of the tree and by abandoning his headship. He had listened to Eve and had not done what he knew was the right thing, and so he too was punished. Now the work God had called him to before the Fall was going to be hard. I would want to argue, with Werner Neuer,[1] that in Genesis 3 we see in the Fall not only humankind rebelling against God, but also the setting aside of the divinely appointed order of man and woman.

I am looking forward to hearing what you have to say as we move on to look at women in the Old and New Testaments. It will be interesting too as we begin to look at how we work out in practice our theology on the role of women. Even within groups that hold the same theological understanding, there is great divergence.

I am both preaching and leading the service on Sunday, which I know would be a problem for some people who hold a similar view to mine on male headship. But for now I can put up my feet, relax and drink a cup of tea as I press 'send'.

With love in Christ
Clare

To ponder
How do you interpret Genesis 1:26–31?
How do you understand the different ways Adam and Eve were created in Genesis 2?
On reading Genesis 2 and 3, do you think headship was part of creation or a consequence of the Fall? What difference does that make?

Pray
Thank God that men and women equally bear his image, and that he calls us into relationship with one another and supremely with him.
Confess the ways in which your relationships are not what they were meant to be.

3. How far can we go? Women in the Old Testament

Suggested reading: Judges 4 – 5; Proverbs 31:10–31

From:	**Lis Goddard**
To:	Clare Hendry
Subject:	Remarkable women

Dear Clare

I hope you enjoyed your well-deserved cup of tea!

There is so much to say about the effects of the Fall on male–female relationships, as we look at the Old Testament and see examples of brutality and abuse generally, and towards women in particular, expressed through rape, murder and prostitution. The distortion of God's original vision of *one* flesh seems to have been twisted into self-satisfaction through **concubines** and **polygamy**. This isn't controversial and I know that you will agree.

In the Old Testament we also see women struggle with barrenness and grief over their desire for children. This is a deep-seated, emotional need, but it is also significantly tied up with the reality that, without children, women often had no social standing or identity. After the Fall, the beauty of the creation mandate to 'go forth and multiply' became dysfunctional, not only in the physical pain now experienced by women, but also in the emotional pain when things just don't work as they should. It also becomes clear that women who were created equally in God's image are now generally defined in relation to men.

Of course there are exceptions to this, such as the remarkable women who, by their piety and deep faith, are an example to Israelite women down the ages: women like Hannah who trusted when there was no hope left, and who put her own needs as a mother second to her faithful discipleship. She teaches us that vital truth that children are never ours. They belong to God, and are entrusted to us to steward. Hannah has certainly been an important example for us in our parenting.

Then there is the Hebrew slave girl in the home of Naaman, who was willing to speak out when her master was leprous, and kept her faith alive even though she was so far from home; and Esther, who through her bravery saved her whole people from destruction. She, like Ruth, is a hero of the faith.

Women were clearly recognized as leaders within Israel from early times. They were not as numerous as the men, but significant nevertheless for their presence and for what they tell us about a society that accepted them. Miriam, Moses' sister, is a good example. In the exodus narrative she is given respect equal to that of her brothers. Exodus 15:20 describes Miriam as a prophet, and she is celebrated as someone who provided key leadership at a pivotal point in Israel's history (Micah 6:4).

Of course, the pre-eminent example of a female leader in the Old Testament is Deborah. She is described in a variety of ways in Judges: prophet (4:4, 6–7), judge (4:5) and mother in Israel (5:7). As judge, Deborah would certainly have heard the cases that local judges could not handle (Deuteronomy 17:8–9). She took over when 'the highways were abandoned; travellers took to winding paths. Villagers would not fight in Israel; they held back . . . ' (Judges 5:6–7), and she restored security. She was a significant commander-in-chief, uniting the tribes and leading them into victory – hence the fact that the victory song is sung both by Deborah and Barak, Israel's general, but her name, as the most significant, is placed first.

Then there was Huldah, a prophet and leader at the time of such prophets as Jeremiah, Zephaniah and Habbakuk. She was consulted by King Josiah when the book of the Law was rediscovered, and as such she must have been a very significant figure. Her words had a profound effect, not only on the king, but also on the whole people of God as they renewed their commitment to the covenant (2 Kings 23:1–3).

Interestingly there is never any suggestion that it was inappropriate for all these women to take on significant leadership roles within the people of God. Indeed, they were leading when there were strong male leaders around too. Of course, alongside this there is the wonderful passage from Proverbs (31:10–31) to which you alluded, praising the industrious, or in our language, the businesswoman.

So here in the Old Testament is a picture of women taking on the full range of responsibilities within the people of God, from mother and provider for the family to judge, leader and prophet, interpreting and speaking the word of God to their generation. The only thing that seems to have been closed to them was the Levitical priesthood, which of course was changed dramatically by the cross.

I love these remarkable women who served God faithfully in what must have been pretty tough times.

With love in Christ
Lis

From:	**Clare Hendry**
To:	Lis Goddard
Subject:	Yes . . . but

Dear Lis

I thought you did a great job in giving such a clear overview of women in the Old Testament. I wish there was more time to explore their roles because, as you point out, there are some great examples for us to learn from, such as Hannah and Ruth.

Like you, I see that the Fall has had a major impact on relationships between man and woman. But I do not think that male headship is a result of the Fall, which is what you seem to be advocating. The way that male headship has operated over the centuries has certainly demonstrated the impact of the Fall. But surely we would expect it to be distorted and spoilt in some way, along with the rest of creation. Where male headship operates more in line with the way God intended, it can be enabling and liberating for the woman. Where I have been under male headship, exercised in a humble, sacrificial type of leadership, I have found a great place in which to blossom in ministry. I have loved being part of a mixed leadership team headed up by a godly man.

I have enjoyed looking at some of the examples of women in the Old Testament. However, as I read the passages, I am not sure that I can come to the same conclusions. For instance, you talked about Miriam receiving respect as her brothers did, but this doesn't mean that she was necessarily a leader on the same level as Moses. After all, surely everyone deserves respect, whatever their role.

You know I have no problem with women exercising some forms of leadership, and I am quite happy to see women taking some types of leadership positions in the Old Testament. But just because something happens in the Old Testament does not mean we can argue that it is always ok. I'm sure you would not advocate polygamy, for instance – not that I am suggesting that women in leadership is in the same category! Furthermore, I would want to argue that women holding various leadership positions in the Old Testament are not exercising the role in the same way as the men do.

Here are a few examples: you quite rightly refer to Deborah as one of the main female figures in the Old Testament, and she is clearly described as a 'judge', 'prophetess' and 'mother in Israel'. I was interested, however, to read your interpretation of what was going on between Deborah and Barak, and how Deborah is named first in the song because she is more significant. I had a different take on the passage. Barak comes across rather as a weak leader, yet he is still the one to lead the troops into battle, urged on by Deborah. So you could argue that she is keen to encourage male leadership! It was because Barak wouldn't go without Deborah that he was told the Lord would hand Sisera over to a woman. Could it be that Deborah's name was placed first in Judges 5:1 as a comment on Barak's behaviour?

Like Huldah and Miriam, Deborah is called a prophetess, but they all seem to exercise their prophetic ministry in a different way from male prophets, such as Isaiah, Jeremiah and Ezekiel, who practised a very public prophetic ministry. Prophetesses seem either to address women, such as Miriam who was followed by all the women (Exodus 15:20), or they spoke in private like Deborah. In their role as judge, their judgments were given to individuals, rather than to a great crowd. Even Huldah spoke only to the five messengers from King Josiah, and in this case I think you give her more credit than she deserves. Yes, Josiah and the people of God renewed their commitment to the covenant, but we already see in 2 Kings that Josiah was a pious man, which was why God was going to spare him the sight of the terrible destruction. It could be argued that it was Josiah who led the people to renew the covenant just as much as the prophetic words of Huldah.

You say that women were leaders even when there was strong male leadership, but in Deborah's time it seems that this was not the case (Judges 5:15–17). I wonder if part of the problem in church leadership today is that we do not encourage men to take the lead, and so women are left to pick up the pieces and assume leadership roles. We see this in missionary history, where at times women seemed more willing to go and be missionaries, and ended up leading churches because there was a distinct lack of men.

But my final comment on Deborah is back to her role as judge. The other judges are all said to have been raised up in some way by God. For instance, look at Ehud in Judges 3:15 or Gideon in Judges 6:14, but in Deborah's case all it says is that 'Deborah, a prophetess, the wife of Lappidoth, was leading Israel at that time' (Judges 4:4). Doesn't this say it all?

I know that some would argue more vehemently against such pictures of female leadership portrayed in the Old Testament. They would be unhappy with any kind of leadership position for a woman. There are probably nearly as many differences within our groups as there are between our groups. I am all for giving honour and credit to the many godly women in the Old Testament, and if we ignore the importance of the role they played in God's work, then I think it is to our detriment. However, I think we can still advocate that, while women and men are clearly created equal in worth, they are created to be distinct in function. Not all positions were open to women in the Old Testament. As you rightly point out, the **Levitical priesthood** was definitely a no-go area for women. You say that the cross dramatically changed this. Obviously now we all have open access to God and are part of the priesthood of all believers, but I think it is a big leap to say that therefore every role is open equally to both men and women. No doubt we will be looking more at that as we move on to the New Testament.

As ever, there is still so much more to say, but this gives a flavour of my comments on the passages.

Hope you get a good break over the holidays. Is Jonathan having to do lots of revision for his A levels? It does seem so much tougher these days – at least we had a bit of the year off from doing major exams. I am trying to encourage Kate to keep her head down in her books as GCSEs loom large.

But whatever our differences, it's great to know that we have so much that is really important in common through the cross.

Look forward to hearing back from you.

With love in Christ
Clare

From:	**Lis Goddard**
To:	Clare Hendry
Subject:	Confused of Bristol

Dear Clare
I am so sorry not to have replied before we went away. There was so much to do as Andrew and I were leading and preaching at a

service. I do love it when we have the chance to do things like that together. I also had a lot of preparation to do – how do teenagers generate so much washing?! I came back to a massive pile of laundry and am just catching up.

If I am honest, my reaction to your email was one of sadness. This surprised me as I usually feel stirred up to work through your points. I found it overwhelming that you felt you had to deny these amazing women their rightful achievements. There aren't many of them in the Scriptures, and it seemed as if somehow their roles were played down and their importance diminished, because otherwise it would be dangerous.

For example, to say that Huldah's ministry was not public surely makes no sense: she was clearly a well-known prophet who was first choice for advice at a critical time (1 Kings 22:14), even over Jeremiah whose ministry had begun five years earlier (cf. Jeremiah 1:2) and Zephaniah (Zephaniah 1:1). So she must have been well established. To draw a distinction between 'public' and 'private' does not fit with the evidence. Five of Josiah's officials went to see her: so this was not a private meeting; it was an official consultation (2 Kings 22:14, 15ff.). Do we dismiss Daniel in the same way because he was seen by the king in a 'private' consultation? It is clear from the text that it was as a result of the prophet's words that Josiah then acted.

I found your treatment of Deborah fascinating. To suggest that she in some sense usurped power and that she was a lesser judge because the language of being raised up by God is not used was bizarre. The whole account of Deborah's time as a judge in Israel suggests the opposite. She is the only judge who is also a prophet (Judges 4:4), surely a powerful sign of God's hand upon her. It is clear too that her prophecies are of God, and that in common with other Old Testament prophets she is filled with the Holy Spirit – one only has to look at the death of Sisera to see that (Judges 4:9, 17–22). I think it would be inaccurate to say that she gave her judgments and prophecies in private to individuals; the NIV describes her as holding court (Judges 4:5). Indeed, the whole scene in Judges 4:4–5 bears a striking resemblance to Moses seated in the wilderness, settling disputes in Exodus 18:13–16, which after all is the type for Israel's judges that follow. Even the Hebrew word order is changed when Deborah is introduced. The normal grammatical structure would be verb-subject, but here her name comes first in the clause: 'Deborah . . . was leading Israel at that time' (Judges 4:4). Thus her significance is immediately established.

It's also hard to see how one can deduce from this that Barak was a weak leader, as the author of the book of Hebrews identifies him as one of the heroes of the faith (Hebrews 11:32), presumably for 'conquering kingdoms'. Clearly he forfeited his final victory to Jael (Judges 4:17–22) by not trusting God's promise 'as spoken through a woman', but that is quite different from being a weak leader. Clearly he was a very effective leader, as he went on to rout the army of Sisera.

As far as the Song (Judges 5:1–31) goes, it is known as the 'Song of Deborah' for a reason. Deborah's name not only comes first, but the verb 'sang' is in fact also in the feminine singular form (Judges 5:1), and the song focuses mainly on Deborah, the one the Lord uses to deliver Israel.

On that note I think I should draw to a close. The sun is shining gloriously outside and I am now really tired.

Hope all is well with you and yours.

Love in Christ
Lis

From:	**Clare Hendry**
To:	Lis Goddard
Subject:	The next exciting instalment

Dear Lis

Thanks for your email. Don't worry about the delay – it sounds like a familiar story. I sympathize with you on the washing front. As I sit to write this, I am surrounded by piles of ironing!

I was sorry to hear your reaction to what I had written. My intention was not to undermine the significance of these women in the Old Testament. Clearly the fact that they are there means they are noteworthy and we can learn from them. However, while women are clearly important, and as much part of God's plan for working out salvation as men are, I do think that the roles women and men play are different.

Sometimes when I make a distinction between men and women, I believe you read that as my saying that women are less significant. So, for instance, when you comment on my observation that the language of being 'raised up' which is used of other judges is not used of Deborah, you say that I am suggesting that she is a 'lesser' judge. (By the way, although you may find the comment on the language of being raised up bizarre, it is an idea put forward by some commentators.) Similarly, you seem to suggest that, by making the distinction between a private or public audience, I am trying to dismiss Huldah. Not at all: in both cases I am making the point that the role is different – being different is not always about greater/lesser or superior/inferior.

Those who hold my position are sometimes seen as trying to undermine the importance and value of women, but that is far from my intention. I want to help those who would agree with me on the subject of headship to understand more of the position held by those who don't, and to encourage them to think more about supporting the training of women for suitable roles in ministry and providing opportunities for them.

I was encouraged the other day to meet Alison, a senior staff member at a church in the north of England which holds a conservative position on male headship. She was using part of her sabbatical to read about the differences between women and men, to think about how that might affect the way they work together on a church staff team and to consider how to acknowledge those differences in practice. Talking to her reminded me of a Church Pastoral Aid Society Ministry and Vocation committee meeting I attended, which was held just before the vote on whether women should be priested (become vicars) in the Church of England. At the meeting, a woman who held a senior diocesan position made the point that for her to get to the position she held she had to learn how to do things in a more 'masculine' way. I think that whatever our differences on the role of women in ministry, you and I both share a desire to see women being able to be fully themselves in the way that they exercise ministry, and not to feel that they have to work in a male way. So I am looking forward to hearing more from Alison.

Let's now move on and engage with the women in the New Testament. We agreed that we would next look at Mary, Jesus' mother, before moving on to other women in the Gospels.

Look forward to hearing back from you

Love in Christ
Clare

To ponder
What light does the Old Testament throw on the role of women in the local church today?

Pray
Thank God for the remarkable women of the Old Testament who followed God's leading against all the odds, and also for those pioneer women of recent times.

4. Changing Times?
Women in the New Testament

Suggested reading: Luke 2:26–56; 10:38–42;
Matthew 12:46–50

From:	**Lis Goddard**
To:	Clare Hendry
Subject:	This is a big one

Dearest Clare

Thank you so much for your last very gracious email. I really hope that mine didn't come across as too strong. I know and appreciate so well that you are committed to women having a ministry for which they are properly trained within the boundaries of your clear position. That's why I find you such a good person to work with, because you take these issues so seriously. However, it is important that I should express the concern I felt. I know that you value the ministry of women and would challenge the contention that difference equals a greater/lesser or superior/inferior dichotomy, but the problem is the way in which it finds its expression within the church in a hierarchy structured around headship. It is difficult to see how equality is the case, but we will doubtless come back to that later when we talk more about headship.

I apologize for using the word 'bizarre' concerning Deborah's calling. I realize that it is a point made by some commentators to highlight that she isn't raised up, though I am bound to say not by others, who point out Deborah's distinguishing role as a prophet, powerfully used by God to lead his people, rather like Samuel, Elijah or Elisha.

It was exciting to hear about Alison and the work she is doing. I would be interested to see it when she is finished. Is she reading mainly theological works or is she also looking at **sociology** and **anthropology**? I too have heard someone talk about learning to work in a more 'male way', meaning a more competitive, hier-archical rather than a collaborative way, I think. While I recognize this attitude as being true of some women and men, it is certainly not true of all. I would have said that the differences between men and women are much less clear-cut and easy to define than we might like them to be.

Anyway, I need to move on, and I must say I am very excited about our first stop – Mary. I love writing about Mary; she is one of my all-time heroes of the faith. We evangelicals can often be almost scared of really engaging with Mary because of the worst excesses of **Mariology** that we see in other parts of the church. But it's so easy to throw the baby out with the bathwater.

I can remember when I was about eleven playing Mary in a school nativity play in the East End of London. This wasn't a trite play; it assumed that we were old enough to understand the nuances of the story and so it acknowledged that Mary wouldn't have been much older than I was at the time. It used her words of total surrender to God, 'Let it be to me according to your word', and in a place of terrible deprivation and human suffering I found myself saying the incredibly prophetic and liberating words of the **Magnificat**.

That was when I began to understand that Mary wasn't just any girl. She was the opposite of Eve, a girl through whose obedience God's salvation entered the world as a baby, just as through Eve's disobedience sin had entered the world. Mary responds to the angel with faith, whereas Zechariah doubted and was silenced for his doubt. In her words, 'I am the Lord's [bond]servant . . . May it be to me according to your word' (Luke 1:38), prefiguring her son's words, 'Not my will but yours'. The Holy Spirit comes upon her

(Luke 1:35), and she not only conceives a child who will be called the 'Son of the Most High' (Luke 1:32), but, like those prophets of old, she is also given a prophetic utterance, which has become a vital song of hope for the people of God down the ages in the Magnificat.

Here is a young girl who knowingly accepts social ostracism and possible summary execution, in a world where marital status and female purity were everything for women. She lives her life knowing that the child she has been given to nurture will tear her apart: 'A sword will pierce your own soul too' (Luke 2:35). We see her later in the drama of the Gospels ostensibly being rejected by her son (Matthew 12:46–50; Luke 8:19–21); and we find her with the women at the foot of the cross, watching her son die when most of his disciples have deserted him.

Mary is a key figure for the Gospel writers: 'His mother treasured all these things in her heart' (Luke 2:51). She is a woman of real sensitivity to the Spirit and to the dynamics of her son's unfolding ministry and authority, as she gently sets the stage for his first miracle at Cana: 'Do whatever he tells you' (John 2:5). It is clear from John's Gospel that, despite Jesus' seeming rejection of her in the other Gospels, she did in fact travel with him for at least some of the time (John 2:12). She certainly seems to have been with the disciples on the day of Pentecost (Acts 1:14; 2:1) when the Spirit came and the New Testament church began.

Mary is a vital player in the divine drama and one whom we ignore at our peril. She is a key signifier of God's redemption, not only of humanity but particularly of women. Here is a woman who got it right. I am not for a second suggesting that she was without sin: she clearly wasn't, nor is she **the Redeemer** (i.e. Jesus), but because of her obedience the incarnation happened. She is the beginning of a key new chapter in the story of God's kingdom breaking in and redeeming what was destroyed by the Fall – the first sign of God restoring creation.

For me, as a woman, Mary is an amazing example and role model. She gives me a fresh insight into what God was doing with both women and men in first-century Palestine, and I want to tell everyone about it!

Well, enough of this high commendation – I am fascinated to know what you make of Mary. She can be such a divisive figure.

With love in Christ
Lis

From:	**Clare Hendry**
To:	Lis Goddard
Subject:	A mother's love

Dear Lis

You are so right about how we evangelicals can react to Mary because of the way other parts of the church have given her almost divine status. I really like the way you link Mary's obedience to Eve's disobedience; I had never thought of it in that way before. A couple of months ago I preached on some of the birth stories and Jesus' visit to the temple when he was twelve. I remember then being struck by what Mary, as Jesus' mother, was going to have to face. The words you quote, 'a sword will pierce your own soul too' (Luke 2:35), are so easy to skip over with everything else that is going on, but how dreadful it must have been for Mary when those words came true.

I don't think I have anything to add to what you have said about Mary. I agree that she is a significant figure in the story of redemption, and you were right to give Mary her own slot. What we can draw from all of that with regard to the role of women in ministry and headship is perhaps to show that women have a great role to play in the redeeming work of God, something on which we both agree – the debate being rather what exactly that is today.

I guess what we need to explore next is the role of some of the other women in the New Testament. I am going to bat this back to you rather than start on it myself, as I am off tomorrow for a few days on a New Wine conference with some of my colleagues from St James's, and I have a son who is beginning to climb up the walls. Typical Bank Holiday weather – it's raining! We are a bit housebound with Kate desperately trying to finish her folder for her art exam on Tuesday and Wednesday, so I need to give Alistair some time.

Love in Christ
Clare

From:	**Lis Goddard**
To:	Clare Hendry
Subject:	This is a big one (part 2)

Dear Clare,
I was glad that you too are excited by Mary – she always inspires me and makes me smile. In our understanding of women in ministry and leadership, Mary is first important for interpreting 1 Corinthians 11 and 1 Timothy 2, but second, I think there is something profound here about God's redeeming work with regard to women: it is vital that redemption is not all about men, and that at the moment of redemption God fills a woman with the Holy Spirit and gives her a prophetic utterance which becomes part of the lifeblood of the church.

As you know, some who take your view of the scriptural passages would deny women any teaching ministry at all, except among children and other women, and yet it is clear from Scripture that this is not how God saw women's ministry. Their prophetic utterances were used and revered by the whole church. Some commentators[1] strongly argue that, by putting the Magnificat in such a prominent position in his Gospel, Luke is making an indirect but clear point about Mary as a teacher of theology, ethics and social justice in the early church. She is a key pivotal figure, a sign of God's original purpose in redemption.

But now we need to move on to the women in Jesus' ministry, and how he related to them. As we look at the evidence in the

Gospels, it becomes clear that, although those named as his twelve disciples were men, this by no means represents the full number of his disciples. Jesus was in fact really very radical in the group he travelled with, and he pushed the bounds of contemporary culture by teaching women, and preparing them for the roles they were to take on in the newly constituted people of God.

I want to start with the incident in Matthew 12:46–50, where Jesus responds to a request from his family, saying, "'Who is my mother, and who are my brothers?" Pointing to his disciples, he said, "Here are my mother and my brothers! For whoever does the will of my Father in heaven is my brother and sister and mother."'

It is interesting here that, following his gesture to his disciples, Jesus then addresses them in male *and female* terms, and includes the word 'sister' which was not there in the question. In a Middle Eastern context, he could not have done this unless there were women present.

Linked to that is Luke 8:1–3, where we read about the conditions in which Jesus travelled:

> After this, Jesus travelled about from one town and village to another, proclaiming the good news of the kingdom of God. The Twelve were with him, and also some women who had been cured of evil spirits and diseases. Mary (called Magdalen) from whom seven demons had come out; Joanna the wife of Chuza, the manager of Herod's household; Susanna; and many others. These women were helping to support them out of their own means.

Jesus is travelling through a series of towns and villages with a group of men and women. At the time this would have been considered socially unacceptable, and yet Luke admits it quite clearly. Given the circumstances, they would all have been regarded as Jesus' disciples, particularly since they were living from the bounty of the women.

The Gospel story of Mary and Martha in Luke 10:38ff. also indicates that Jesus had female disciples. This has to be one of my favourite Gospel stories: it makes me laugh and I always feel that it is so permission giving. I really understand Martha, but it's wonderful that Mary is loved and accepted so much. The key to this story is that Mary is at Jesus' *feet*. Sitting at the feet of a rabbi meant that you were his disciple: thus Paul describes himself as having been brought up at Gamaliel's feet (Acts 22:3). It is not surprising that Martha is distracted from Jesus' teaching by the cooking and by her sister, who is bringing shame on the household by sitting among the men as a disciple of the rabbi.

Jesus' response is very telling: he knows what Martha is worried about, and responds that what Mary has chosen is good. In other words, it is good for a woman to be a disciple, to sit at Jesus' feet with the men, and it will not be taken away. This is totally radical in the culture of the time, when women were not able to study and learn, and had little value.

I want to move on to the reinstating of women within the **kingdom of God** throughout Jesus' ministry. You may ask what this has to do with ministry and leadership, but I want to look at how redemption brings the **new creation order**, the reversing of the effects of the Fall, as I would understand them. This is worked out concretely in the fact that Jesus made the effort to talk to women at a time when it was frowned upon for a man to speak with a woman in public. Furthermore, he had serious conversations with women on a par with the one he had with Nicodemus – deep theological discussions which would have been considered unsuitable for women.

We have the example of the Samaritan woman at Jacob's well, whom no one else cared about and who was ostracized by society. Indeed, she was almost certainly a person who had been greatly sinned against, possibly because of her inability to bear children (John 4:1–42), and therefore was handed on from one man to another. Yet Jesus turned her from an outcast into the first great evangelist: 'Many of the Samaritans from that town believed in him because of the woman's testimony' (John 4:39). This remarkable story shows what Jesus was doing to release women from the bondage of sin and its effect on their lives, not just in terms of rescuing them from a life of ostracism, but also by giving this woman, and all women, a voice and a role in sharing the gospel.

Similarly, the remarkable account of the woman caught in adultery challenges our understanding of the pervasiveness of sin and causes us to question the prevailing gender stereotypes and power games of the day. How interesting that the only one to be 'caught in adultery' is the woman and yet, by its very nature, adultery is a sin involving two people. Where was the *man* caught in adultery? Jesus does not accept the status quo, the unquestioning condemnation of the defenceless woman; he holds the mirror of God's expectation up to all those standing there and makes it clear that all have sinned – none is perfect and all need redemption. He is gentle where the scribes and Pharisees are brutal, and restorative where they are destructive.

The same is true in so many other Gospel stories: for instance, the woman who wept over Jesus' feet and dried them with her hair, a blatantly erotic and shocking action, and yet he did not reject or condemn her. His reaction was always one of acceptance and restitution.

But perhaps for me the primary example of God's remarkable redemptive work through Christ for women is what happened at the resurrection. If anyone had told those first followers that it would be God's purpose that women would be the first witnesses of the resurrection, they would have laughed and would not have believed it. In fact, for me this is one of the key things that assures me of the authenticity of the Gospel accounts. No first-century Jew would have written such an account of an event and attempted to convince others by basing the evidence on the testimony of women. And yet this is precisely what happened in the Gospel narratives. Despite the fact that a woman's evidence was not valid or acceptable in court, it is absolutely clear that Jesus appeared first to women, and it was they who had to go and tell the disciples that he was risen. They were not only the first witnesses, but they were the first conveyers of the truth. What is more, they were specifically commanded by Jesus to go and tell the others what they had seen and to convey his words to them (John 20:17; Matthew 28:9). The Gospel writers were not ashamed to record this.

Jesus here commissioned the women to step outside their expected roles, to take the lead, to teach and to break the conventions. They had been disciples of Jesus during his life, they had been witnesses of the resurrection, and now they were commissioned by Jesus to go and spread the good news. In essence they are apostles in the wider New Testament sense of the word. The destructive power of the Fall has been overthrown. It seems to me that here in this nugget we have a vital truth about the new creation order which God is ushering in with the redemption won through the death and resurrection of Jesus.

Yesterday I listened to an amazing exposition of 1 Timothy 2:8–15 by Emma Ineson, who is on the staff at Trinity College here in Bristol. I do love that passage! Emma is ordained and was talking about how liberating and important it is to be under Scripture and under the authority of God. It was so inspiring, especially as I looked around at all the women there who are training for ordination. It is wonderful to know there are so many women out there who are partnering in the gospel and struggling like us with God's Word.

With so much love as ever in Christ
Lis

From:	Clare Hendry
To:	Lis Goddard
Subject:	Here's another one!

Dear Lis
It was great to talk on the phone the other day and catch up with each other. Kate has now finished her GCSEs, so we will be celebrating that as a family on Sunday. Hope the end of exams is

looming soon for your household, if it hasn't happened already. Roll on the summer – I am struggling with a grotty cold and feeling very much in need of a break.

Gaz, our new **curate**, is moving in this coming week and will be ordained at the end of June. I look forward to working with him in some of the pastoral areas of church life. I much prefer working in a team than on my own, which is why, I guess, Jesus sent both the Twelve and the Seventy-two out in twos – we just aren't meant to work on our own.

I really enjoyed reading your latest email. There was a lot to think through, and once again so much on which we do agree. I do hope that, whatever position people adopt on headship, etc., after reading this book, they will take women's role in ministry seriously and see how women can best serve God within the church.

I am intrigued about what you said about Mary and how she can help us understand women in ministry and leadership. I am totally with you that redemption is not all about men – all of humankind is fallen and in need of redemption. After all, Christ our Saviour came into the world through a woman, to save all humankind – male and female. But having said that, I cannot see how that necessarily says anything about headship – either way. The Magnificat is certainly an important part of the Gospel, and Mary's role is hugely significant in God's gracious act of salvation, but I can't see how you then make the leap to saying that Mary is somehow to be regarded as a teacher in the early church.

In arguing against those who say women should teach only children and other women, a view certainly held by some who take my position on headship, you say that it is clear from Scripture that is not how God saw women's ministry. But surely part of the reason why we are having this debate is because for many it is not clear. Indeed, some would say the exact opposite, and argue that it is clear from Scripture that women should not teach men. Let's unpack that more when we come to look at the relevant passages in chapter 8.

I was very interested to read what you say on the reinstating of women within the kingdom of God in Jesus' ministry. I see it more as evidence of how Jesus valued and respected women, and why it is so important to value women in ministry, rather than as an argument against headship. The significance you draw from all of this rests on how one understands the effects of the Fall. As we have said, you see male headship as being a consequence of the Fall, whereas I see it as being part of the original created order. In order to get a clear picture of the type of headship that was intended before the Fall, we need to look to Jesus to see how he led his disciples and how he interacted with people. If anyone has the right to headship with authority, it is Jesus! And yet, in his willingness to die for us on the cross, we see that he modelled a servant type of headship.

I think you may be reading too much into the Matthew 12 passage. I must admit that I had never come across your take on it, and on rereading it I was still unsure. So I headed for the commentaries, but they seemed to shed no further light. My New Testament Greek is very rusty, but from the English translation surely Jesus is saying that **messianic mission** takes priority, even over family loyalties. I would read the addition of sisters as just showing the inclusiveness of God's people, and referring to whoever does his will, whether male or female.

It certainly seems likely that women were travelling around with Jesus as part of the larger group, as you indicate from such passages as Luke 8:1–3. It's possible that some were even wives of the disciples. Now at one level you could quite legitimately say Jesus had women disciples, if you are using that term to indicate general followers of Jesus as opposed to the twelve disciples. However, I think it is clear from the specific references to the Twelve, sometimes called **apostles**, that they were exclusively male.

Much of what you say shows the importance of women for Jesus. He goes against so much of the normal teaching within Judaism, which treated women as second-class citizens. For instance, his teaching on marriage and divorce is remarkably unbiased (Matthew 5:32; Mark 10:11–12) in a culture and religion which had such double standards for men and women. As we have been preaching through Luke at St James's, we have seen how so many of the stories show Jesus putting men and women on an equal footing, starting right back with Simeon and Anna, two righteous Jews who praise God on seeing the Christ child – there is no hint of Anna having a lower status than Simeon.

Jesus is so countercultural. You see it time and time again, especially in the way he treated such women as Martha and Mary. What has never yet been adequately explained to me by anyone is that if Jesus was so countercultural in the way he treated women (which I don't doubt), why were the twelve disciples he chose all men; why not choose some women among that group? After the resurrection why not take the opportunity at the beginning of Acts to replace Judas with a woman? Why does it say that it was necessary 'to choose one of the men who have been with us the whole time the Lord Jesus went in and out among us' (Acts 1:21)? Surely there would have been women among the larger group who could qualify, if it hadn't been specified that it must be a man. Similarly, with the choosing of the Seven in Acts 6 where there was a problem with some of the widows being over-looked, the Twelve assembled all the disciples together to choose 'seven men from among you who are known to be full of the Spirit and wisdom' (Acts 6:3). Now I can't imagine that there wouldn't also have been women in that group, who would not equally fit into the category of being full of the Spirit and wisdom, and yet we are told that the Twelve specifically asked for seven men.

It was amazing that Jesus chose women to be the first witnesses of his resurrection, but I can't see how you can then infer that Jesus commissioned these women 'to step out of their expected roles to take the lead, to teach and to break the conventions'. To be sure, they were breaking with convention in being witnesses to such a world-transforming event in a culture where female witnesses did not count, but how a simple command to go and tell 'his brothers' (which from the other Gospel accounts seems to be the disciples) commissions them as leaders and teachers beats me.

Anyway, no doubt you will have lots to throw back at me (in a nice way!). I guess we should now move on to women in the early church in general. It always seems a shame to move on, as I think we both have more to say. But on the other hand, we want to leave a few trees standing! Do let me know if you are heading this way in the next month or so. It would be good to meet up, especially as I will be away during the summer – hopefully sunning myself in the States where we are visiting various friends.

Well that's enough from me. Hope you and yours are all well. Look forward to hearing back from you soon.

With lots of love in Christ
Clare

From:	**Lis Goddard**
To:	Clare Hendry
Subject:	Lots of leading ladies

Dear Clare
Thank you so much for your last email – it was good to hear from you and to know that the dreaded exams seem to have gone off all right. I hope you all enjoyed your family celebration! Things here haven't been so straightforward. Jonathan went down with a virus towards the end of his exams; he is still not well and is now worried about the work he is missing, not to mention the further maths. It seems like the pressure is never off. I shall be very glad when the summer comes and they can have a really good break!

I am sometimes surprised by where you and I don't agree. It is interesting to see what things matter to me, but don't seem to have the same significance for you. For example, I do not feel that we can rush straight at the 'headship' question without first looking carefully at the context. This is why it is so important to establish the significance of Mary and the women who travelled with Jesus, or those with whom Jesus had dealings. They are links in a chain as a whole new way of being is established, and they set the context against which we need to read everything that follows. For you I think this does not appear to be as important, except as a sign that Jesus valued women and their ministry, which feels a bit woolly to me. You are quite right in your analysis that my whole understanding is rooted in my reading of Genesis and thus the restored creation order that comes with redemption.

I can see that my statement about Mary being a teacher could have seemed a bit left field, but I am not the only one to take that view. Perhaps we need to ask how the stories of Jesus would have been communicated, if not by his mother, and what the implications are of the church giving such significance to the Magnificat.

It also seems clear that women taught. We need only look at Acts 18:2–26, Romans 16:3, 1 Corinthians 16:19 and 1 Timothy 4:19 to discover Priscilla who, along with her husband Aquila, is referred to by Paul as his co-worker in Christ who risked her life for him (Romans 16:3). Paul seems to have known this couple well, given the number of references to them in his letters. We know that he travelled with them and stayed with them, and they shared his trade, tent making. But it would seem that they were also willing to put their own safety on the line for Paul and 'the churches of the Gentiles'. They were clearly well known and held a key leadership role, not least in the leading of a church in their home (Romans 16:5). Linked to this, and perhaps more significantly, we discover Priscilla teaching Apollos with Aquila in Acts 18.

This is interesting for a number of reasons. Priscilla is named first of the couple. As you know, this would have been pretty much unheard of at the time in all the surrounding cultures, where the man's name always came first. Paul and Luke (writing Acts) would only have changed it for a very good reason. In this instance it seems likely that Priscilla was the more significant partner, quite possibly therefore taking the lead in the teaching. Clearly she was not just a tag-on. We can see something similar happening even today, where the same social convention is still largely the norm. We can tell from our Christmas cards which part of our lives someone comes from. If the cards are from those who have primarily known my leadership or teaching ministry rather than Andrew's, they will address them to 'Lis and Andrew', rather than 'Andrew and Lis'.

We must assume that this was not basic teaching for beginners. Apollos was already theologically literate: 'a learned man with a thorough knowledge of the Scriptures. He had been instructed in the way of the Lord . . . and taught about Jesus accurately, though he knew only the baptism of John' (Acts 18:24–25). Thus the teaching he received from Priscilla and Aquila must have been advanced, showing the depth of their theological education. This demonstrates not only that Priscilla was allowed to teach men and that no one disapproved (indeed it was accepted), but also that she herself was well educated, not least in the ways of the Lord – an unusual thing for a woman at the time. No wonder Paul speaks of the couple so highly and with such affection.

Of course, there is the important question of whether it is permissible for women specifically to preach, which I know some who take your position would consider unacceptable. Some folk I know would be happy with a woman as college lecturer in theology or even biblical studies, but would draw a very firm line at preaching. It is an interesting question because most of the New Testament examples of preaching are basically evangelistic in character, and I am not aware of anyone who would forbid a woman from preaching evangelistically. Indeed, as I mentioned in my last email, the Samaritan woman in John 4 is an example of a woman doing just that, and the women witnesses of the resurrection were commissioned by Christ to do that too, but I will return to this later.

It also seems likely that the women deacons in the early church, like their male counterparts, found themselves preaching and teaching, although I suspect that our rather nice distinctions would not have made sense to them. An interesting example of this is Phoebe, who is described by Paul as 'deacon of the church in Cenchrea' (Romans 16:1–2). We know that those who were described as deacons in the New Testament preached and taught. Indeed, Paul describes himself as a deacon (Ephesians 3:7; Colossians 1:23, 25) and he uses the same word (*diakonos*) of Timothy (1 Timothy 4:6). With Timothy it is clearly a position of some significance within the church in Ephesus, which involved teaching, discipline and oversight. Despite its beginnings, this would appear to have become a recognized role within the early church, reflecting something of the ministry of Jesus.

Obviously we cannot be sure what Phoebe did, especially as this is the earliest example we have of someone being given the *title* of deacon. It does appear, however, that she was a significant figure in the church in Cenchrea, with a definite ministry and leadership role. She is also described by Paul as someone who 'has been a great help to many people, including me' (Romans 16:2 NIV). The word translated here 'been a great help to' is *prostasis*, which should be translated as 'a woman set over others; a benefactress or guardian'. Phoebe has generally been regarded as a benefactress, someone who provided hospitality to the saints, including Paul, in the sea port of Cenchrea.

However, there may have been wider implications. From what we read in Romans 16 it would appear likely that Phoebe was the deacon entrusted with transporting Paul's letter to the church in Rome, given that she is the key person whom Paul commends to them. To all the others in chapter 16 he sends greetings. If she carried the letter for Paul, then it is quite possible that, as Paul's representative, she would have been called upon to explain (i.e. teach) the letter to them. Indeed, this may have been the context of Paul's request that she be given 'any help she may need'.

You said in your last email that my interpretation of the significance of the choice of women as first witnesses of the resurrection 'beat' you. You could not see how their commission by Jesus to go and tell the disciples could in any way be seen as breaking down the old barriers. I understand that, but I hope you will consider what was actually going on, and the link that can be drawn between them and Junia in Romans 16 to whom I will return shortly.

At the end of the Gospels we see these women being commissioned by Christ to 'Go and tell . . . ' Yes, it is initially to the disciples, but it seems odd to suppose that their witness would have ended there, or was intended to finish there. I find it hard to imagine that they would have been able to stop themselves from witnessing to others about what they had seen. I have never yet met a new Christian, male or female, who could limit themselves to telling their story just once!

Indeed, there is a parallel between the encounter of the women with the risen Christ in Matthew 28:8–10 and that of the disciples in Matthew 28:16–20. In both passages their response is to fall down and worship him, and on both occasions they are commissioned. Clearly in the second passage just the eleven are present, but that does not negate the impact of the first encounter. Indeed, I would argue that it needed to be just the eleven at that point, for exactly the same reason as Jesus originally chose twelve male disciples: the Twelve represented an enacted parable. Here Jesus is signalling that, in him and his mission, Israel is being reconstituted and redefined. Twelve male disciples represented the twelve tribes of Israel – the **old covenant** – and now in him, following his death and resurrection, all that is changing. Thus, on his ascension he commissions the Twelve to 'go and make disciples of all nations' (Matthew 28:19). The old Israel with its dividing lines has been broken down, and the new Israel is beginning in Christ.

Something similar is happening with Christ's commissioning of the women to 'Go and tell my brothers' (Matthew 28:10): old divisions are breaking down and women are becoming witnesses and learning to speak and to take a lead. Perhaps the most obvious place where this happens is in John's Gospel where, after meeting with the risen Lord, Mary Magdalene goes to the other disciples and says, 'I have seen the Lord' (John 20:18). Here is a clear parallel with the language used by the disciples when they relate their encounter with Christ to Thomas: 'We have seen the Lord!' (John 20:25). It would appear to be the expected declaration of both witness and revelation, and therefore signifying apostolic identity. Furthermore, there is an echo here of 1 Corinthians 9:1, where Paul writes of the qualification of apostle: 'Am I not an apostle? Have I not seen Jesus our Lord?' It seems that there were two different uses of the title 'apostle' in the early church: first of all, to designate the Twelve, and second, to signal those who had a clear ministry of witness and leadership linked to their direct appointment and commissioning by the risen Christ in the period following his resurrection.

Paul himself fell into the latter category (although, because of the nature of his commissioning, he placed himself slightly outside it – 1 Corinthians 15:5–8), as did Barnabas (Galatians 2:9; 1 Corinthians 9:5–6), Silvanus (1 Thessalonians 2:6–7) and several others (doubtless some whose names have not been recorded like much in the early church). This brings us to Andronicus and Junia in Romans 16:7, whom Paul describes as his relatives – possibly meaning that they were Jews like him. Here we discover a key woman. Andronicus and Junia are described by Paul as 'outstanding among the apostles'. The word here translated as 'outstanding' in the NIV and TNIV can perhaps be more properly rendered as 'prominent', and so Paul describes this woman as 'prominent [or outstanding] among the apostles'. This is surely very important as we explore whether women should be allowed to take on roles of leadership within the church. There can be little doubt of the importance of the apostles in the early church. Indeed, Paul writes of the church being 'built on the foundation of the apostles and prophets' (Ephesians 2:20).

This would seem to confirm that Paul acknowledged the existence of female deacons / church leaders, teachers and apostles in the early church, and in his final chapter of Romans he appears to have no problem with them. Indeed, he commends them to the church for their self-sacrifice and service to the gospel.

Alongside all of these, we have the example of Lydia (Acts 16), a very wealthy and therefore culturally significant woman. She is a dealer in purple cloth which was more valuable than gold! Following her conversion, she brings her whole household to be baptized and then opens up her home for the gospel. She is the first Greek convert and, as head of the household, she invites Paul into her home, and so the Greek church began to grow. Lydia's home probably became the first 'church' in that context.

Another woman who held a church meeting in her house is Nympha, mentioned by Paul in Colossians 4:15–16. We are not told much about her, except that Paul specifically greets her, and there is a link between her house church and the church in Laodicea, so we can assume that it is based there. As Paul mentions her specifically and she is described as having a church meeting in her house, it's a fair assumption that she is also the leader of that church, as indeed we assume Philemon to be on the basis of Philemon 1.

Of course there are specific references to other women in the New Testament, such as Chloe (1 Corinthians 1:11), Lois and Eunice (2 Timothy 1:5–7), not to mention Euodia and Syntyche (Philippians 4:2). But I think I have said enough for now, and I should hand over to you to respond.

With lots of love in Christ
Lis

From:	**Clare Hendry**
To:	Lis Goddard
Subject:	Leading ladies?

Dear Lis
Good to hear back from you. How's Jonathan? I was sorry to hear about his virus – exams certainly seem relentless nowadays. Anyway, I hope you all manage to get a good break over the summer.

Now to business. Once again you have sent me a lot to get my teeth into.

You mention that the roles of Mary and other women who travelled with Jesus don't seem as significant for me as they do for you. Mary was an important figure and certainly played a part in passing on stories about Jesus' life. Certain verses in Luke seem to indicate that he knew Mary and obtained some of his material from her, such as Luke 2:51.

I certainly don't want to come across as downplaying the role and valuable contribution of women in the church. I do think Jesus was countercultural, and we see that in how he treated women, which is why I pointed out last time that, since he was often countercultural, there was surely nothing to stop him including women in the twelve disciples!

I agree that you can argue strongly from Scripture that women are involved in ministry, which includes prophecy and some teaching (whether that is just of women or includes men as well is open to debate by some) among other things, but I am still to be convinced that Scripture advocates women leading a church. In some ways I wish I could agree with you, but I don't think the evidence is as strong or clear as you suggest. Rather than go through each instance, I've selected a few of the key examples you gave.

Concerning Priscilla and Aquila, you quite rightly say that when they are mentioned as a couple Priscilla's name sometimes comes first, which was unusual for that culture and so could indicate that Priscilla was the more 'significant one'. You follow that up by stating that she was quite possibly taking the lead in the teaching. Well you may be right, but perhaps it was significant for a different reason. In those days when women from a higher social class married a man from a lower social class, the name of the woman would sometimes be placed first. So I don't think we can definitely say which is the correct explanation as to why Priscilla is *sometimes* mentioned first. Furthermore, the teaching that Aquila and Priscilla did was in private in their home, so while it is clear that Priscilla was an intelligent and well-educated woman who taught alongside her husband, again I think it is a big jump to say that women can therefore lead a church.

The more I look at these passages and others, the more I think that women were involved in some teaching, which is a position I have always held, and on which we both agree. We definitely need to look more closely at this area and what women were doing, before we focus on whether women can head up a church, and we need to tease out more of what the Scriptures are teaching. Passages such as 1 Timothy 2 present almost as many challenges to me as to you, since I do teach both men and women publicly. Things get complex as we seek to draw out principles from Scripture and apply them. As you mention, there are some who might be happy with a woman teaching theology in a college, but not preaching. However, in my experience many who draw the line at women preaching would also not be happy at women teaching the Bible in college.

Those who don't believe women should preach would, if they are being consistent, also say that evangelistic preaching is unacceptable. However, I am sure they would be happy with a woman giving her testimony. Was the Samaritan woman in John 4 preaching? Surely she was just sharing the good news of what Jesus had told her – more testimony than preaching, which is more to do with opening up God's Word and applying it to the listeners' lives.

I am sure that we will come back to this as we examine various New Testament passages. You pick up on the issue of deacons. Did women serve as deacons in the New Testament period? It may well be that Phoebe was a deacon. But I must admit that I am unsure about this. Many Bible translations have 'servant' in Romans 16:1, but include a footnote that it could also be translated '**deaconess**'. In this passage Paul's emphasis is more on Phoebe's service rather than on the office of deacon. 1 Timothy 3:1 may also mention women deacons, but again many versions translate this as 'wives of deacons', although the possible translation as 'deaconesses' is noted in some footnotes. However, even if it is clear that women served as deacons, we must then ask a further question: What implications does this have for making a case for a woman to head up a church? Surely the New Testament makes a clear distinction between the office of **elder/overseer** and that of deacon, as we read in Philippians 1:1 and in the more extensive passage in 1 Timothy 3:1–13. Part of the confusion that exists today may arise from how the various denominations use those titles. In some churches deacons are on the governing body of the church, and their role is closer to that of an elder than of the New Testament style deacon. The two qualities of an elder – being able to teach/ preach (1Timothy 3:2; Titus 1:9) and overseeing or governing the church (1 Timothy 3:5; 5:17; Acts 20:28) – are not required of deacons.

What might be confusing is that some deacons, such as Stephen and Philip, who were appointed as part of the Seven in Acts 6 to take over some of the duties of the Twelve so that they were free to concentrate on the 'ministry of the Word', also seemed to be doing things that were not regarded as the normal role of a deacon. In Acts 6:8 Stephen 'did great wonders and miraculous signs among the people' and preached powerfully (Acts 7:2–53), and Philip opened up the Scriptures to the Ethiopian eunuch (Acts 8:35).

Two points to say on that. First, although it seems that most people think of these seven as 'deacons', the actual title of 'deacon' is not used in this passage in Acts 6. The verb *diakonia* (verse 1) is used to refer to the need, and the verb *diakonein* (verse 2) is used with reference to the tasks that need to be fulfilled. However, despite that, these men were probably appointed as deacons. My other point is that Luke features Stephen and Philip just because they were exceptional men, who did more than was expected of a deacon.

It would be a cop-out if I didn't engage with what you wrote about apostles, and about Romans 16:7 in particular, where Paul is sending greetings to Andronicus and Junias, whom he describes as being 'outstanding among the apostles'. Some scholars have questioned whether Junias is actually a shortened form of the male name Junianus. Even if this person is a woman, further clarification is needed as to her position in the early church. She was obviously a woman of great significance and was highly thought of by Paul, but was she an apostle in the way we normally think of that office?

It's not easy to get your head around this. Some scholars argue that the verse can be read in a different way, and that Paul is actually saying that they were outstanding in the eyes of the apostles. I am uncertain either way, but we do need to acknowledge that it is open to debate.

What is more important is to examine more closely the use of the term 'apostle', and see how it was used in the New Testament. It is by no means clear that Paul was giving Junias the same position as the Twelve or James (1 Corinthians 15:7; Galatians 1:19). The term *apostolos* is not always used as a technical term, as we see in 2 Corinthians 8:23 for instance: 'As for Titus, he is my partner and fellow-worker among you; as for our brothers, they are representatives [*apostoloi*] of the churches and an honour to Christ'; and in Philippians 2:25: 'But I think it is necessary to send back to you Epaphroditus, my brother, fellow-worker and fellow-soldier, who is also your messenger [*apostolon*], whom you sent to take care of my needs.' The word *apostolos* is used in a different sense here and hence is not translated as 'apostle'. Sometimes it is used in a non-technical sense to refer to itinerant missionaries, which may well be the case in Acts 16. There is little evidence here to show that Andronicus and Junias were leading a church. So I don't think that from this brief verse one can build a strong case for women apostles in the sense of the Twelve or James, who clearly did have authoritative teaching and oversight positions in the early church.

Well, there is so much more that could be said, but we need to move on to look at Galatians.

I have just booked for the **AWESOME** conference, so I will at least see you there, but hopefully we could meet before then.

Over to you for the next instalment.

With love
Clare

To ponder
On reflection, what do you think were the various leadership roles of the women mentioned in the New Testament?

Pray
Thank God for the faithful women, like Mary, who took great risks for him.
Ask God for wisdom to understand how to relate what you have read to your life and ministry.

5. 'All men are equal . . .'
Unpacking Galatians

Suggested reading: Galatians 3 – 5

From:	**Lis Goddard**
To:	Clare Hendry
Subject:	And so to Galatians

Dear Clare

Thanks for asking about Jonathan – yes, he is much better now.

Moving on, we agreed to start with Galatians, which is reckoned to be one of the earliest books (if not the earliest) in the New Testament and therefore a really sensible place to begin to explore Paul's teaching. The verses that are usually cited in this debate by those who take my position are Galatians 3:27–29, focusing particularly on verse 28:

> For as many of you as were baptized into Christ have put on [clothed yourselves with] Christ. There is neither Jew nor Greek, there is neither slave nor free, there is no male and female, for you are all one in Christ Jesus. And if you are Christ's, then you are Abraham's offspring, heirs according to promise. (ESV, with my expansion on the Greek text)

It is worth beginning by putting this in context. Galatians is a letter written by Paul to the church in Galatia primarily to help them to get straight the earth-shattering implications of the gospel. Paul has planted the church, and then left them. They have been led astray from Paul's original teaching about freedom in Christ and are beginning to teach that those who are not Jews have to be circumcised in order to belong. Thus the kingdom which Christ ushered in becomes not something radical and new, but really just more of the same – a chance to be disciples of just another radical rabbi / teacher within Judaism.

Needless to say, this was not what Paul with his apostolic authority preached, and it is absolutely not where he wants the Galatians to remain. The whole letter is devoted to helping them to discover the really significant implications of what he taught when he was with them, and how it would work out in practice. This is not the place for a full exposition of Galatians, but we must remember that these **proof-texts** do not stand alone, and need to be understood and interpreted within their context.

The key things to understand are that if the Gentile or Greek converts accept the case for circumcision, then they must also accept everything that goes with it – specifically the bondage of the **Mosaic Law** which has been broken, and from which all humanity have been freed by Christ. As Paul says in Galatians 3:23, 'Before the coming of this faith, we were held in custody under the law, locked up until the faith that was to come would be revealed.' So this is the point of Galatians 3:27–29: Paul is working out for his readers what that freedom from custody looks like in Christ.

This is a passage about salvation – no debate there either I am sure! We read in verse 26, 'in Christ Jesus you are all sons of God, through faith' (ESV), that is, not just the free Jewish men, but all of you; 'If you are Christ's, then you are Abraham's offspring, heirs according to promise.' Inclusive versions of the Bible often change 'sons' here to 'children', but actually it is important to retain the word 'sons', because in the society of the day only the boys were able to inherit. Paul is saying that, in the new kingdom which Christ has inaugurated, inheritance is totally equal and there is no differentiation. In terms of salvation, the uncircumcised Gentile, the slave and the woman all stand on an equal footing with the free Jewish man.

What is interesting, however, is that Paul is not just concerned with our individual salvation, but also with what this means for us corporately, and then with how this works out in practice. He therefore, slightly surprisingly in the context of the passage, goes on to speak of the baptism of believers and how they have 'put on' Christ – a metaphor for the transforming power of Christ at work in their hearts and minds, which changes the way they approach everything. Nothing could be the same again, for they are clothed in Christ, which symbolized the baptismal rite of the very early church where new converts changed their clothes. They are now new creations in Christ, and this concept of the new creation is key to understanding what comes next.

Paul sees the young Christian community as something new and dynamic; the old has gone and the new has come. In them God is working out his purpose of redemption, not just for individuals but also for the world and creation – hence Paul can finish his letter to the Galatians with the words, 'Neither circumcision nor uncircumcision means anything; what counts is the new creation' (Galatians 6:15). The damage done at the Fall has been overcome in Christ. The relationship between God and humans is put right and creation is being restored; there is a new creation – creation as it should have been. But – and this is the key thing that Paul draws out in Galatians 3:28 – it is not only the relationship between God and humans that is put right. When our relationship with God is restored, it inevitably affects relationships within the body of Christ: 'There is neither Jew nor Greek, there is neither slave nor free, there is neither male and female, for you are all one in Christ Jesus.' Suddenly the implications of the new creation become abundantly clear, and it is not very comfortable for those who like things to be bound up with structure. The sociological categories no longer count: now it is how we live within the categories that is all-important.

There is much I could say about this, and clearly the key category for Paul's readers was that of Jew and Greek, but for our purposes I need to focus on the final pairing of male and female, and what

Paul is doing by including this here. There are several things to note. First of all, in the other places where Paul makes similar pairings (1 Corinthians 12:13 and Colossians 3:11) the male/female juxtaposition is not included. So why is it here? And why does he use the words that focus specifically on the gender distinctiveness of the sexes, rather than the standard words for man and woman which he would normally use? Finally, why does he break the flow of the pairings which in the Greek have gone 'neither . . . nor . . . neither . . . nor . . . ' to make the stark change to 'neither male and female'. This change is particularly obvious in the Greek. Paul did not have to add this final pairing, so he must have done so for a reason. It must have been relevant to his purposes. So the question is – why did he do so?

Paul was writing to a culture that would have inevitably fostered and emphasized a deep inequality between men and women (as indeed it would between both the circumcised and uncircumcised, and the slave and the free) because of the teaching about the need to follow the Mosaic Law. So the addition of this pairing fits neatly with his argument, countering the Judaizers and pointing to the new creation in Christ. Women were excluded from Jewish circumcision, and by virtue of their monthly periods they were regularly rendered unclean, and were therefore excluded from various parts of Law observance required by the men. If the Christian community in Galatia accepted this teaching that led to them following the Law, they would, as far as Paul was concerned, regard their women as second-class citizens. Paul is at extreme pains to counter this. He breaks down the distinctions between male and female in the new creation which exists in the body of Christ, just as he later writes to Philemon instructing him to accept Onesimus back as a brother rather than as a slave (Philemon 16).

I suppose it is rather like the gentlemen's clubs in London. I remember visiting one as a child: it was grand and beautiful, and I was quite dazzled. I wanted to explore it all. But then I realized that I was allowed only in the ladies' part – it was very luxurious and comfortable, but my brothers could go further in and discover the rest, in particular the libraries. As an adult I went back to the same club and found that they had opened it up to women and I could go everywhere – I could read all the books and explore all the rooms. If someone were to come along and suggest that the old rules should be reinstated, it would be a similar situation to the one Paul faced.

So it would appear that Paul is here saying that there will still be men and women, but the false sociological differences of dominance are irrelevant within the kingdom. They may impinge outside, and indeed men and women will bring diversity to the body as each brings their gifts to the table, but 'you are all one in Christ Jesus' (Galatians 3:28). This is very similar to the body language repeated elsewhere in Paul, interwoven with the language of the **new creation**.

So here is Paul saying that all the old barriers which were imposed as a result of the Fall have been broken down, and that God is restoring creation, and specifically male–female relationships, to the mutuality and harmony which was originally intended. We see this remarkably worked out elsewhere in the New Testament, obviously through those women whose leadership and ministries we read about, but also through Paul's injunction in 1 Corinthians 7:3–5, for example, where he speaks to husbands and wives on absolutely equal terms in marriage. This is totally out of keeping with anything else in the ancient world.

So alongside the reversing of **Babel** and the challenging of the post-Fall structures of slavery, Paul also challenges the hierarchy which entered the world after the Fall. No one who accepts today Paul's challenge to live the kingdom life, where there is neither Jew nor Greek, slave nor free, does so suggesting that we should see that as a purely spiritual salvation injunction. Yet when it comes to the male and female part of the clause, so often everything changes.

It would appear that the early church, while struggling to live within its social context, was actually pretty radical as it lived out its own calling to be the kingdom of God on earth.

Well, I think I shall hand this over to you, and get on with preparing for the teaching on leadership I have to do next week. This week's session is on working in teams, which I am so passionate about. I lead this group with three great guys. We are all very different and yet we work together really well.

Hope all is well with you and yours.

With much love in Christ
Lis

From:	**Clare Hendry**
To:	Lis Goddard
Subject:	Gripped by Galatians

Dear Lis
Good to hear from you. I have just been reading about the ordinations in *The Church of England Newspaper*. It's great to see that, despite all the problems within the Church of England, men and women are still coming forward to serve God through it. Gaz, our new curate, was one of the ordinands featured – generally a great article, but I'm not sure how he is going to feel about the typo which says he is aged sixty-six!

Thanks for starting off the section on Galatians. I think this is a great passage, but perhaps not for all the reasons that you think it is. The main issue that it addresses is one that we have just been exploring in Philippians in our ladies' Bible study group ('Thursday Focus'). It has made me realize how easy it is to be very critical of the **Judaizers**, who wanted to add things and thus deny the heart of the gospel, which is justification by faith, and not by obedience to the Law. But we too can be guilty of adding our own things to what makes a 'proper Christian' – that they need to believe this or that, or take this or that position on issues such as headship, and we forget what really unites us – the gospel.

And now let's get on to looking at the passage. We pretty much agree on most of it but, as with other passages we have explored together, our application differs. That's because we have a different understanding of what happened at the Fall in Genesis. You say that 'in Christ the damage done by the Fall is overcome' – absolutely – something we can really celebrate! But if you start from my position, that the roles, hierarchy or order (or whatever we call it) between man and woman were there before the Fall, as ordained by God, then there is nothing to put right, apart from the way in which that role difference has sometimes been abused in practice.

I have consulted various commentaries (whose authors' Greek is far better than mine), and they don't draw out any particular point from the original Greek wording. I am not sure if Paul was trying to signify something by his choice of words, but we must also read this in the light of other passages where Paul does seem to say that there is a difference between men and women.

As you say, Paul clearly did not have to add this pairing, but he did so and for a reason. We agree that at the time Paul was writing there was a deep inequality between men and women within both the Jewish and Gentile cultures. I remember hearing about a common morning prayer that some Jewish men would pray: 'I thank God that thou hast not made me a woman.' This passage certainly addresses such prayers.

When you spoke about Paul breaking down the 'distinctions between male and female in the new creation which exists in the body of Christ', I wasn't clear what distinctions you were referring to. Is it the 'false sociological differences of dominance' which are now irrelevant within the kingdom because, as you say, all the old barriers imposed as a result of the Fall are broken down? If so, I agree. In the new creation the negative impact of the Fall upon male-female relationships will be dealt with, and the relationship which God created between them will be restored. I see the 'dominance' you speak of as part of the Fall: women have sometimes been treated badly because some men have abused their position of headship.

The context for Galatians 3:28 is surely about faith in contrast to law as the primary means of salvation. Paul is teaching that, whatever our race, social status or gender, we are all justified by faith (verse 24), we are all children of God (verse 26), we have all put on Christ (verse 27), and all are heirs according to the promise (verse 29). There are none of the normal barriers in society which divide God's people. But the thrust of this passage is about oneness in Christ rather than equality (although that is also true). Paul is not writing about some future time when all of this will be true, when those distinctions will be done away with and when, for instance, slaves will be free. He is writing about a present reality. Believers are already united in Christ and clothed with Christ because of what has already happened – they already have oneness in Christ. All have equal access to salvation. And when you consider the way slaves, Gentiles and women were treated by many in those days, that is radical.

I have a few more things to say about the passage in relation to other teaching in the New Testament, but I want to hear what you think about what I have said so far. As with other passages, we will probably end up by saying, 'Well, we will have to agree to disagree.' But I'm sure we will stand together on the great news that this passage declares, which is that we are all one in Christ, whatever our position, status or gender,.

Look forward to hearing back from you. Hope you have a good week.

Love in Christ
Clare

From:	**Lis Goddard**
To:	Clare Hendry
Subject:	Galatian equality

Dear Clare
Thank you so much for your careful and swift response. I am aware that we are now pressed for time with the summer holidays looming! I have just had a very busy week. Andrew has been away

all week and I have had to attend meetings in London and Durham! It has left me feeling really tired, particularly when combined with juggling all the other everyday things, such as taking Nell to a hospital appointment, getting her ready for an exchange trip to France, and helping Jonathan to think through why coming in at 2 am when you have agreed to be home by midnight may not be the most responsible thing to do! The joys of life with teenagers . . .

But back to our discussion. I do find it interesting that there are times when we seem to be saying the same thing and then suddenly we veer off in totally different directions!

For example, I couldn't agree with you more when you say that Paul is writing about a present reality – the interesting thing is how we then perceive that present reality. If I understand you correctly, you would see it in spiritual terms. In other words, this is about the fact that 'all have equal access to salvation', and that this is solely about justification by faith. I would totally agree that this passage is about equal access to salvation, and that is indeed radical. However, I would contest that that is *all* it is about. I think it is much richer than that. Equal access to salvation has consequences in the here and now.

If all have equal access to salvation, then all have equal access to Christ, all have equal access to the inheritance in Christ and all have put on Christ. Salvation has implications, and the implication is the ushering in of the kingdom of God. The Christian community is *meant* to be countercultural, shocking to the culture around it, a place where a slave-owner such as Philemon can be asked by Paul to receive his runaway slave as a brother; where Jew and Gentile live and eat together with no distinction; where uneducated fishermen become leaders of the church; and where women are welcomed into teaching and leading roles. This is a church where all have equal access to salvation, and so all are welcome to serve within the church. Salvation is not *just* about me and my individual relationship with Jesus – it changes the whole way I relate to the rest of God's world, because I am being transformed into the likeness of Christ.

re in Paul's letters we see that the early church becomes a piace wnere leadership is determined not by sociology, but by gifting, and gifting is not gender specific. The ground for this is first laid at the very beginning, in Acts 2:17–18:

> And in the last days it shall be, God declares,
> that I will pour out my Spirit on all flesh,
>   and your sons and your daughters shall prophesy,
> and your young men shall see visions,
>   and your old men shall dream dreams;
> even on my male servants, and female servants
>   in those days I will pour out my Spirit, and they shall prophesy.
> (ESV)

Paul constantly speaks in terms of the gifts that God has given for those who will lead the church, and at no point does he suggest a gender limitation on these. Thus we have the list in Ephesians 4 of **apostles**, **prophets**, **evangelists**, **pastors** and **teachers**, which is preceded by the verse which says that 'he ascended . . . and gave gifts to humanity' (my translation: the Greek word *anthrōpos* is best understood as the generic term for 'humankind', rather than 'men'). All these gifts are, as we have seen, ones which were given to women in the early church.

In 1 Corinthians 12 there are the lists of what are often referred to as the more 'spiritual gifts'. Again there is no hint here that women are forbidden from exercising them; indeed, Paul has just said in 1 Corinthians 11 that he expects a woman to pray and prophesy (but we will come on to that in chapter 6). In Romans 12 there is the other significant list of gifts. Here again, as in Ephesians and 1 Corinthians, it is couched in the 'body-metaphor', which is surely key to understanding Paul's concept of the church. It is a metaphor of total mutual dependence: 'In Christ we, though many, form one body, and each member belongs to all the others' (Romans 12:5). Here again, there is no gender limitation; indeed, the only limitation given is that of grace: 'We have different gifts, according to the grace given to each of us' (Romans 12:6). He then goes on to provide a list of gifts which are different from those in either Ephesians or 1 Corinthians, and examines how they should be employed.

Perhaps the most interesting gift listed here is that of leadership in Romans 12:8. Paul uses the same root word here as he does later in Romans 16:2, where he describes what Phoebe does. But whereas here it is always translated as 'to lead/preside', in Romans 16:2 it is always translated as 'to be a great help' or 'to be a patron'. (In fact, it is also the verb Paul uses in 1 Thessalonians 5:12 to refer to those who are set over them in the Lord.)

Clearly, there is also much that we could discuss about the interrelatedness, or otherwise, of prophecy, preaching, teaching and leadership. It seems clear that there were female prophets, not only in the Old Testament but also in the early church. Acts 21:8–9 speaks of the four unmarried daughters of Philip who prophesied, and in 1 Corinthians there is the positive expectation that women will do so (1 Corinthians 11:5). Indeed, we have seen when Paul speaks of spiritual gifts in Romans, 1 Corinthians and Ephesians, there is no suggestion that this is just for men.

My point in looking at this gifts language has been to explore something of the groundwork laid down in Galatians 3:28. The new Christian community was to be and, from our reading of the New Testament, was (though with teething problems) a place where God was doing something new and radical. It was a place where the kingdom of God was breaking in and the new creation order was being established. The early church didn't always get it right, but it wasn't good enough for them to continue owning their brothers and sisters as slaves, insisting that their Gentile brothers should be circumcised or excluding their female members from *full* participation in the body of Christ. We would not expect to return to that way of living today, as we recognize that it is in no way consonant with the gospel.

Anyway I think that is probably enough from me on Galatians – especially if you are to stand any chance of getting off on holiday this summer. Have a lovely time in America; it makes Yorkshire and Northumbria seem quite dull by comparison ☺, although actually I am sure we will have a wonderful time with dear friends and in beautiful places! I can't wait.

With love as always in Christ
Lis

From:	**Clare Hendry**
To:	Lis Goddard
Subject:	Grounding Galatians

Dear Lis

Thanks for getting back to me so quickly. It means that I can respond before we go off next week.

I can totally empathize with you on your conversation with Jonathan. We have had similar conversations, and I guess we will have many others in the years to come. I think being a parent has tested my Christian faith more than most things, although it has also helped me grow in it. Parenthood has given me an amazing insight into God's love for us as our Father. No matter how hard our children push us, we still love them, even if at times liking them is more of a challenge.

Back to Galatians. We are so much in agreement on the subject of the welcoming of women into teaching and leading roles. However, who women teach, in what capacity, and in what kind of leadership role and so on, is more open to debate. Within the group that take my position on male headship, there is a great diversity in working out how the Scriptures are applied. Some are happy to see women teach mixed congregations (as long as it is clear that they are under the authority of the male vicar), whereas others think women should not be teaching men at all. No doubt that will come out more as we go on to look at some of our remaining passages.

I am totally in agreement that salvation is not just about the individual and their relationship with Jesus, but it transforms the way we relate to all of creation. But you then go on to say that in the early church leadership comes from gifting rather than sociology, and gifting is not gender specific. If we were to view leadership only in terms of gifting, I might have to agree with you, and that would mean a massive shift for me in how I regard women in overall leadership roles. However, as I look at other Scriptures, starting with Genesis, I see distinctions in the roles to which men and women are called, and sometimes in the way they are to use their gifts.

So yes, women clearly have teaching gifts, and God is not going to give gifts to people without providing them with the opportunity to exercise them – that clearly would be absurd. At the very least women can certainly teach other women. In fact, I would want to go further and say that they can teach mixed congregations within the local church, as long as it is done in a way that supports overall male headship.

However, I can't quite see how you arrive at your conclusion from Acts 2 and Ephesians 4, where Paul refers to some being pastors, some being evangelists, and so on. We have already agreed that there are some women prophets, and that women did play a part in the early church. For instance, we have already looked at Priscilla and Aquila together teaching Apollos, but I have yet to see where there is a clear example in the New Testament of women fulfilling a **pastoral office** or being involved in regular public teaching in the local church. I think it is a big jump from being gifted to saying therefore we as women can have any role that uses those gifts, as there are passages which seem to indicate that the overseer of the local church should be male. It is precisely because the New Testament is so countercultural that surely there would be clear examples within the early church of women leaders overseeing the local congregations, if that is how it was meant to be.

We agree that God gifts both women and men. I think that, in churches where there is a more conservative view on women's ministry, there is sometimes so much discussion on what women can't do that not enough effort is made to help them discover their gifts and give them opportunities to exercise them within the local church. Within our women's Bible study groups we are making a few changes for the autumn which I hope will help women to discover their gifts and have a chance to use them, perhaps in leading the worship or a Bible study, or in offering hospitality.

I have spent time ploughing through the passages you mention and looking at what the commentaries say, in case I have missed anything that might lead me to think again on women overseeing local churches, but I can't find anything conclusive. For instance, with regard to Phoebe I can see no clear evidence that she was leading the church. Wayne Grudem[1] has an interesting section on the use of *prostatis* and its verb form *proïstēmi*, and whether it just means 'patron' or, as some try to argue, signifies 'to stand, place before or stand over'. There is much written about Phoebe's position in the church from both sides of the debate. Some focus on whether she was a deacon or not. On looking at the relevant passages, it is unclear, but even if it was to be shown that Phoebe was a 'deacon' as opposed to a 'servant', as some translations have, the passage does not indicate that she had any teaching or governing authority in the local church. However, I do agree with R. C. Sproul[2] that she clearly had some kind of ministry in the church at Cenchrea.

I can see what you are saying about Galatians 3:28 and how the gifts language lays the groundwork for a new Christian community. I am with you on that, but as I look at the whole of Scripture, I can't see how some of the passages (such as 1 Timothy 2 and certain passages in 1 Corinthians) fit in with the picture of everything being open to anyone, regardless of gender. Within all the equality and distribution of gifts of the Holy Spirit, there does seem to be an order and a call to different roles for men and women – roles which together serve and glorify God. The difference in roles certainly does not mean that women are inferior in any way, but just that we are called to different jobs and giftings. (By the way, sorry about using the term 'roles'. I know it bugs you! But it is what I think God is laying down in the early chapters of Genesis.) Full participation in the body of Christ is in no way undermined just because people are fulfilling different roles. In the same way, a man who is an 'ordinary' member of the congregation and using the gift of hospitality is in no way less valued or seen to be not fully participating in the body of Christ just because he is not an overseer.

I am struck by Romans 12:2: 'Do not be conformed any longer to the pattern of this world, but be transformed by the renewing of your mind.' I wonder if, in a bid to counteract the terrible injustice done in previous generations to women, who were treated in many areas as second-class citizens, we have at times gone too far along with society today. In a bid for equality, we want equality of roles as well. I have no problems with that in any arena except in the family and in the local church, which is where I think Scripture does make a distinction. I hope to show that as we look at later Bible passages.

As I reread what I have just written, I realize that, while I may receive applause from some, I may also have outraged many readers. I am not trying to be offensive and I do respect those who have reached a different position from mine on headship after a careful study of Scripture. I don't think it is always clear, as people will see as we email each other back and forth. However, I have to be faithful to what I think Scripture is teaching – hopefully with the humility to admit that I am not infallible.

We need to move on. Next stop 1 Corinthians. I will be in touch soon with my first thoughts on that.

Love in Christ
Clare

To ponder
If we have 'clothed ourselves with Christ' (Galatians 3:27), how do you understand what difference this will make to us as Christians? Do you think that God orders his church primarily according to gifts or roles?

Pray
Thank God that in Christ we all have equal access to him.
Pray to know how to live this out in your life and in your community.

6. Hats off?
Sifting 1 Corinthians

Suggested reading: 1 Corinthians 11:2–16 and 14:26–40

From:	**Clare Hendry**
To:	Lis Goddard
Subject:	In at the deep end!

Dear Lis

It's great that we have finally been able to fix a time to meet up when I get back from the States. I do hope that you get a good break over the summer as well. I just have to get things tied up at St James's before I head off.

Years ago at seminary, I remember writing an essay on 1 Corinthians 11 and 14, which I have just dug out and reread. It was the first time I had begun to think about the role of women in the church. Since then I have done a lot of thinking and, while my views may have modified a bit, I still remain convinced of my initial stance.

1 Corinthians was written to address various problems within the Corinthian church which gave rise to disputes. Many of those areas are ones that we still need to address today. Paul deals with both theological and practical problems. He addresses serious **doctrinal** disputes and moral sins, as well as problems in Christian living, including disorderly conduct in worship.

The key passages are 1 Corinthians 11:2–16 and 14:26–40, and are part of a section within the letter from 11:2 – 14:40 which looks at divisions over corporate worship. Within these passages are some intriguing verses on head coverings / headship and the silence of women in church. The passages are theologically complex and raise all kinds of issues. At first glance they seem to be making a distinction between men and women, whereas in Galatians the focus was on unity and doing away with differences. It's in working out the meaning and application of such passages that has led you and me to different positions.

As we look at the section beginning at 1 Corinthians 11:2, Paul starts off by commending the Corinthian church. But it seems that some women were abusing their Christian liberty by being unveiled in public worship meetings, which was offensive to both Jews and Gentiles. Paul, by his use of *de* ('now') and not *peri de* ('now about'), shows that he is not taking up one of their questions, but is introducing a new subject, one that is relevant for their situation. He then goes on to address head coverings by talking first about Christ: 'The head of every man is Christ, and the head of the woman is man, and the head of Christ is God' (verse 3). This is the divine hierarchy of headship.

Paul goes on to say that men should pray with uncovered heads, but women are to have covered heads. Why the difference? Well, some commentators think it was to make the men distinct from Jews who prayed with their heads covered, but evidence seems to point to this practice originating in the fourth century AD. Paul then goes on to say that man is not to be subject to any creature, and a covered head is a sign of subjection – hence, the woman who is under subjection is to cover her head. Much of Paul's argument for women wearing a head covering is bound up with the issue of her husband's authority, and it was the custom in those days for a married woman to have her head covered. Fortunately, even if you were to take this view, I think the equivalent of showing subordination in today's culture is not hat wearing, which is great as I look terrible in hats!

Paul goes on to give his reason for a man not covering his head: 'since he is the image and glory of God' (1 Corinthians 11:7b). Paul's view of man and woman is derived from Genesis 1:26, 27. He applies being made in the image of God specifically to male as opposed to female, because Adam is her source and Eve was made from Adam's rib. Paul also says that woman was made for man and not the other way round. Paul is not denying the equality of the sexes, but he does talk about their diversity. By taking his proper place under God, man glorifies God, and a woman is the glory of her husband as she stands in a proper relation to him and demonstrates that role in reality. Lis, I can imagine you shouting out at this point that woman was also created in God's image. But I am with Morna Hooker,[1] who accounts for Paul's lack of discussion about woman being created in the image of God as just not relevant here. Paul further bases his judgment on the reaction of the angels (verse 10). So a woman should not only think of the reaction of men to her conduct, but should also consider the angels.

In this context 'authority on her head' is to be taken as a reference to her husband's authority. Paul then goes on to talk about man and woman and their dependence on each other. A woman may be under the authority of man, but that does not mean that she is in her very nature of less value. I really like the picture that Paul paints here: when men and women are working together in the roles God has ordained for them, they complement one another and draw out the best in service for God.

We also need to look in a little more depth at the role of prophecy and teaching as it relates to headship, and to define what we mean by prophecy. The term has a variety of applications. It can be used of anything from some spontaneous outburst to what amounts to a carefully planned and worded speech.

In the Bible both men and women prophesy, so it seems that it was acceptable for both men and women to proclaim what they believed to be a message from God. However, there is a difference between prophecy and teaching. You could say that preaching has an element of prophecy in it: after all, it is about proclaiming God's Word. But it is more than that, in that those who preach use the gift of teaching in their exposition. I don't think we should equate prophecy with the regular preaching and teaching of God's Word to his people.

Paul goes on to advise the Corinthians to judge for themselves (verse 13). He seems to be saying that they should reach their own conclusions without instruction from him. In his closing section he works his major themes. Human beings should give glory to God by being what God created them to be. Long hair (or some kind of head covering) is a sign of womanhood, of her glory, but it is a disgrace for a man. So Paul finishes by stating very firmly that it is the universal custom in the church for women to cover their heads.

The big debate here is what does *kephalē* mean (the word used for 'head' each time in 1 Corinthians 11:3). One suggestion is 'source' or 'origin' (in the sense of the source of a river), and I guess this is the meaning you would favour. A second meaning is 'leadership' or 'headship'. Apparently there is also a third interpretation: 'ruler of a community', but this is much rarer and seems an unlikely reading in this context.

I recently read an appendix by Wayne Grudem[2] which looked at the use of *kephalē* as in the sense of having authority, and the number of examples where that was the case in both biblical and ancient secular sources was very convincing. While I am prepared to acknowledge with others that 'head' may mean 'source' in some instances, there are many examples of the word clearly being used with the meaning of 'authority'. When we react against the word 'authority', I wonder if this sometimes comes from our rebellious nature, a consequence of the Fall, and society's strong emphasis on individuality and autonomy. Despite believing in the biblical basis of headship and authority, I know my initial reaction is still to kick against it.

How can it make sense to read 'head' as 'source' in Ephesians 5:22ff. for instance, where Paul writes about the husband being the head of the wife as Christ is the head of the church? I can understand that Christ could be regarded as the source of the church, but in what way is the husband the source of the wife? It makes more sense to read it as 'authority', as Paul goes on to call wives to be submissive to their husbands. He also uses 'head' with the meaning of 'authority' in Ephesians 1:22, and says that God raised Christ from the dead, seated him at his right hand far above all other authorities and powers, 'placed all things under his feet and appointed him to be head over everything for the church'. The focus on the exaltation of Christ suggests that 'head' is used in the authority sense. No doubt we will look at some of these things in greater detail when we come to Ephesians.

Going back to Paul's use of the relationship between Christ and God is clear evidence that the relation between Christ as head over man, and man over woman, is not a cultural thing and not a result of the Fall. Paul is not making Jesus subordinate to God – there is no difference in nature between the Father and the Son, but rather the Son willingly submitted himself to the Father's authority.

These are just a few thoughts to get you going. There are other things that I haven't looked at yet, such as what it means 'to be the glory of', but I thought it was probably the right time to stop and hear what you have to say. The challenge of these passages is to do justice to them without getting bogged down in too much detail – no easy task! We also need to look at 1 Corinthians 14, which again deals with worship. It says some interesting things about women being silent in the church, which on first reading seems rather at odds with the fact that in chapter 11 they are to pray and prophesy.

Have a good summer

Love
Clare

From:	**Lis Goddard**
To:	Clare Hendry
Subject:	Exploring the depths

Dear Clare
Thank you so much for your reply to my last instalment on Galatians and this wide-ranging introduction to 1 Corinthians! You

won't be surprised to know that I don't agree with how you read the text – but I hope you will be pleased to hear that I haven't been shouting at the computer!

I hope you had a wonderful holiday in the States – we had a great time in North Yorkshire and Northumberland. We structured it around visiting York and Durham Universities for Jonathan. I am so grateful that we have teenagers who still want to come on holiday with us. I think the best bit was the final evening when we shared and prayed together – what a privilege!

But I must move on with you to 1 Corinthians 11 – you have given me a lot to respond to. Thank you for your helpful introduction to the passage. I think the best place to start is with the thorny question of what Paul means when he uses the word *kephalē* ('head'). This is absolutely key for understanding not only this passage but also so much else of what Paul says about male-female relations. You rightly assume that I do not agree with you in taking the meaning of *kephalē* to be leadership or headship; but in fact neither would I argue that it means 'source'. There seems to be little evidence for it either within the text or externally, although I know others from my position would disagree. I want to suggest a third way.

As you say, it is important to place this passage within the context of all that follows, but I think it is equally important to see it within the context of what has gone before. So often we see the chapter divisions in our Bibles and, indeed, the big paragraph break between verses 1 and 2 of chapter 11, and we easily forget that these were not placed there by Paul, but by later **editors**. This can lead us to think that the passage we are considering is somehow a completely new thought and unrelated to what has gone before. I am convinced that a careful, continuous reading of the text is the key to a proper understanding of our passage.

So 1 Corinthians 11:2–16 follows on from a long section where Paul has been discussing how believers should view their freedom in Christ. This would appear to be the root of the problem in Corinth: the believers have discovered, possibly through hearing similar teaching to that in Galatians, that they are free, and now they are exercising that freedom in a way which is not compatible with the gospel. So Paul here tries to help them to understand what gospel freedom means. Thus he can say in 1 Corinthians 9:19: 'Though I am free and belong to no-one, I have made myself a slave to everyone, to win as many as possible.' It is within this context that he writes in the verses immediately preceding our passage: 'For I am not seeking my own good but the good of many, so that they may be saved. Follow my example, as I follow the example of Christ' (1 Corinthians 10:33 – 11:1).

There are clear echoes here of Philippians 2:3–11, where in that great hymn Paul writes:

In humility count others more significant than yourselves. Let each of you look not only to his own interests, but also to the interests of others. Have this mind among yourselves, which is yours in Christ Jesus, who, though he was in the form of God, did not count equality with God a thing to be grasped, but made himself nothing, taking the form of a servant [Greek: 'slave']. (ESV)

It is against this background that Paul moves on to his discussion of the Corinthians' disorderly worship. Of interest is the fact that he begins, as you point out, by commending them, although it is not clear what exactly he is commending them for, apart from the 'traditions'. Given the context of what he goes on to discuss, this presumably refers to the fact that both men and women are praying, prophesying and leading the people in worship. He is now writing to help them to change their attitudes to one another as they do this.

In 1 Corinthians 11:3 Paul goes on to say: 'But I want you to realise that the head of every man is Christ, and the head of the woman is man, and the head of Christ is God.' But what does this mean? There are various things to notice – first, this is not written in a way that suggests that Paul is talking here about leadership or hierarchy of any sort. If that were the case he would have written thus: 'The head of Christ is God, the head of every man is Christ and the head of woman is man.' This does not appear to be what he is doing, which immediately suggests that he is not using *kephalē* in this way.

There is no sense here in which Paul can be said to be establishing a 'divine hierarchy of headship'. This is hardly surprising, as this statement comes at the beginning of a passage where Paul uses the word *kephalē* again and again to speak of the part of the human anatomy at the top of the body. This passage is the prelude to a whole section which at various points deals with how to handle Christ's body in communion appropriately, and also how the church should behave as the body of Christ.

I know that Grudem has done a wide-ranging study of the **semantics** of *kephalē*, but I think that I am with Perriman and Thistelton,[3] who maintain that the evidence for it meaning 'chief' or 'leader' in the **Septuagint** and other ancient literature is very thin. Indeed, the strongest evidence for its use is as a metaphor for the head,[4] expressing 'the dimension of visibility, prominence, eminence, social superiority, not the other dimension of authority and subservience for which other terminology was available' (Perriman).[5] The only reference in the passage to authority comes in verse 10, which the majority of commentators take to mean not a sign of the husband's authority over the woman (as you suggest), but of her own authority. I will return to this in a later email when we look at this part of the passage.

It seems clear that Paul is using body language here, and we have to understand it in the context of all the other body language references, as well as what he has said about what it means for Christ to be the 'head'. Paul tends to be consistent in his use of language, particularly within one passage. He has just told us that we are to imitate him as he imitates Christ; he now tells us, by implication, that Christ is his head. So what does it mean for Christ to be head of man – or indeed for man to be head of woman? Our clue is in 1 Corinthians 10:33: 'For I am not seeking my own good but the good of many, so that they may be saved.' It is this mutuality and self-giving love which surely sums up the dynamic within the Trinity, and which Paul is commending to the Corinthians as the bedrock of their relationships. We do not seek our own good; we seek the good of others – Christ's dynamic is salvation. So we conclude that when Paul moves his argument on to speak of Christ being the head of every man, he is talking about a dynamic wherein Christ is pre-eminent and supremely models self-giving and self-sacrifice for us, as Paul outlines in Ephesians 5:25–33. This is not about leadership and authority; it is about giving all we have for the other. It is about relating to one another.

I think Paul's point is that men, who were created first, and clearly creation order is significant here, should behave towards women as Christ does towards men, towards his whole church, and indeed towards the world – giving himself sacrificially for the sake of salvation. Those who come first have an obligation to model sacrificial love to those they are given. This does not mean that they should automatically take authority over the other: the whole point of this passage in context is that as Christians we should not stand on our rights or demand our freedoms. In fact, this little verse, which has caused so much controversy over the years, is really there in many ways to set the scene for Paul as he moves on to challenge the Corinthians on their disorderly worship. As we move through the rest of the passage, the issue of how they, and particularly the women, are to use their freedom surfaces again.

Yes there is a difference between men and women, as we shall go on to explore, hence the structure of this verse – as C is to B, so D is to C, and B is to A. This particular relationship is not reciprocal: only the man is head, or foremost in the sense of being the first. But the head cannot survive or function without the body, and it is only when both function well that the body as a whole is healthy. Indeed, in Jewish thought the head was not understood to be the controlling organ as it is today.

I know there is much more to say on this passage, and I need to go on to look at the questions of head coverings, honour/dishonour and glory – not to mention the angels! But I think I have written quite a lot and I want to give you the chance to respond before I move on.

I am really looking forward to seeing you on Monday. It will be so good to meet up and chat this stuff through face to face.

With so much love as ever in Christ,
Lis

From:	**Clare Hendry**
To:	Lis Goddard
Subject:	Coming up for air

Dear Lis

It was good to chat face to face about how things are going with the book. Great to finally meet Nell and Jonathan having heard so much about them. I hope Nell had a good time at Soul Survivor. Alistair is on a **CYFA** camp. I think those camps can be so important in helping youngsters grow in their faith.

I was interested to hear of your third option for what *kephalē* means. I am totally with you on the importance of reading things in context. However, I have to disagree with your argument that Paul is not talking about leadership or hierarchy. The order of 1 Corinthians 11:3 certainly strikes one as rather odd at first reading, but it makes perfect sense if Paul is leading up to giving commands to men and women. Surely it is natural to refer first to the one who is the head of men and women, and then draw the comparison between Christ and God. Certainly that is the view of commentators such as Blomberg.[6] I am not saying that this passage is just about headship, but I think that it does imply certain things about headship, within the context of how believers should exercise their freedom in Christ and conduct their worship.

I still don't see how you fully explain the order of verse 3, although you refer to Ephesians 5 in backing up your point. When we come to discuss that passage, you will see that I strongly disagree with your reading of it, since I think Paul clearly does talk about leadership there, but I do like your emphasis on relationality. Whatever terms we use, leadership or authority are surely also about relationships. The dynamic within the Trinity is a great model for us, but it is also a model where there is submission (but that is probably a whole new discussion).

I don't quite follow your point about how the 'body language' is used. The use of body language throughout the Bible is varied, so the following passage in 1 Corinthians 11 on the Lord's Supper speaks about the bread and wine reminding us of Christ's body and his sacrifice, but then in chapter 12 the body is used as a picture of the whole church and how we form different parts of the body, as all parts are needed for the church to function properly.

I agree with all you are saying about seeking the good of others, mutuality and self-giving love, but I don't think a reading of headship from this passage disagrees with this at all: it actually fits in very well. In Colossians 2:10 Paul describes Christ as the 'Head over every power and authority', and yet he gave up his life to save others. I think we are often resistant to male headship, because we see it exercised in a flawed way. We see some men use it in a dominant way, and yet it works so well when it is exercised in the way that Christ does – sacrificially, wanting the best for his people over whom he is the Head. I was reflecting the other day about various male 'bosses' I have had (even the word 'boss' seems to have rather negative connotations). Those who have exercised leadership in a more godly and servant-type way have been so much easier to work with.

Another thing I want to mention is what you said before moving on to look at 1 Corinthians 14. In your argument against this passage being about male headship, you say that the only reference to authority comes in verse 10. Well, the only word meaning authority is there, but I think there are references to authority/headship in other ways in the passage. You say that the majority of commentators do not take it to mean a sign of the husband's authority, but the commentaries that I have read on this passage clearly take the view that it was a sign of the husband's authority. So it would be fairer to say that among evangelical scholars there is a disagreement on the interpretation of this verse.

It is amazing how we can both read this passage, both with a clear commitment to the authority of Scripture, and yet come up with a different understanding and application. But there is also so much we do agree on. I think what has struck me as we work together through these passages is that at the end of the day the most important things are gospel issues. The subject of headship and other such topics are certainly important, especially since they have implications for how we do ministry, but we shouldn't lose sight of what is most important of all – the message of salvation.

Anyway, moving on to the second passage in 1 Corinthians (14:26–35). In chapter 12, Paul addresses the subject of spiritual gifts. I love his emphasis on how all gifts are important, and that together they work to edify and build up the body of Christ – the church. Then we have the well-known chapter 13, which looks at the importance of love in the exercise of the gifts. I guess that resonates with how I feel leadership should be exercised. In chapter 14 Paul begins by dealing with a situation in the Corinthian church where some believers were elevating the gift of speaking in tongues above all the other gifts. In the second half of the chapter he focuses on the need for order in worship because, as he says in the final verse of the chapter, 'But everything should be done in a fitting and orderly way.'

Verses 33b–35 rather leap out at me! It might have helped if Paul had not written, 'As in all the congregations of the saints', because then we could say it obviously refers to a specific situation in the Corinthian church, and doesn't generally apply to the rest of God's people today, but Paul is applying these verses to all the churches. So in verse 34 he says, 'Women should remain silent in the churches. They are not allowed to speak, but must be in submission, as the Law says. If they want to enquire about something, they should ask their own husbands at home, for it is disgraceful for a woman to speak in the church.'

Has Paul lost the plot? Is he contradicting what he has said in earlier chapters where it seems fine for women to pray and prophesy? Does this mean that I have to stop preaching and leading the services or prayers in church – it would certainly cut my work load! Lis, I know you, like me, believe that Scripture does not contradict itself. So what is going on here?

I have just ploughed through a selection of commentaries, and at one level I am no wiser. There seems to be a wide divergence in interpretation, from those who say that women should not speak in a public service (I am not sure whether that means they couldn't read the lesson or lead prayers), to those who suggest that these verses are talking about women chattering during the meeting, and maybe asking questions which would be better dealt with at home. Some commentators even say that Paul didn't write these verses, but that they were added in later. I went on to read various other authors who have written on this passage, and again came across a variety of explanations. I could go through many of them, but that would take a lot of space, and I think it would be better to suggest that as follow-up reading for anyone who wants to delve deeper.

As we all do, I will be bringing my own world-view to the passage, but I guess that is inevitable as we try to let Scripture interpret Scripture, and we are influenced in our reading by how we have understood other passages. The challenge is to keep an open mind and not let one's own agenda overly influence one's reading of the passage.

One approach to this passage that does seem to make sense to me is proposed by a few authors, including D. A. Carson.[7] In chapter 11 Paul does clearly seem to say that women can prophesy and pray (although some views say that Paul does not indicate that this was in public meetings). However, the point that Paul is making here is that women should not be weighing up public prophecies. I think it is the responsibility of all believers to listen to what is said publicly in a service, whether it be preaching or prophecy. But the ultimate responsibility, especially if there is disagreement in the church, over whether something is correct must surely lie with the leadership team, and in particular with (in the Anglican setting) the vicar, minister or pastor, who in my view should be a man. I am still not totally convinced of this interpretation, but I am certain that somehow the passage is speaking about lack of submission, which was causing shame to be brought on the church.

In his argument Paul mentions the Law and seems to refer back to Genesis 2:20b–24, the same verses he uses when discussing the role of women in 1 Corinthians 11:8, 9 and 1 Timothy 2:13. When we looked at Genesis, I argued that it laid down a creation order and relationship between man and woman, and submission between a husband and a wife. Here in the context of worship, it seems that women were disrupting the service by their lack of submission, which was in some way shameful and possibly bringing the church into disrepute. I could say more about this, but I think it's time to hear from you, and no doubt I will have a chance to say more in my reply. Besides, my brain is really beginning to hurt!

The end of the holidays is fast approaching, and I am already starting to pick up work things. So I will finish now and make the most of what is left of my holidays. I hope you have/had a good time with your parents.

With love in Christ
Clare

From:	**Lis Goddard**
To:	Clare Hendry
Subject:	Not drowning but waving?

Dear Clare
Thank you so much for your latest offering, which I have read this morning after packing Nell off to school – one down, one more to go! The children had a great summer, packed full, and they are now going back to school for a rest I think! Nell came back from

two weeks' camping, first at Soul Survivor and then at Lee Abbey, with a nasty cough, so she has needed lots of TLC. Jonathan has been frantically trying to do all his school vac work in five days – nothing changes there then!

As ever, I enjoyed reading your piece. I do understand where you are coming from and I totally agree that in some sense this issue is secondary, and that salvation – or the gospel – is the most important thing, but I think it has wider implications. I do emphatically believe that the crucial thing is for women and men to come into a living, life-changing relationship with Jesus Christ, a relationship that brings salvation through repentance and forgiveness. This is non-negotiable. But I passionately believe that when women and men are brought into a living relationship with Jesus, he also calls them to be involved in ushering in the kingdom of God on earth – 'your kingdom come . . . on earth as it is in heaven'.

Like you, I have worked with and for some very godly men – and some very ungodly ones too. So this does not prove the argument one way or the other. I have also worked with godly women, who were servant leaders of both men and women just as much as the men I have worked for, and again I would not want to say that it proves the argument one way or the other. For me, the key question is not whether men or women can live up to this calling of leadership, but whether, scripturally, that is their calling under God.

As I dealt with only the beginning of chapter 11 in my last email, I want to have a look at the rest of it before moving on to 1 Corinthians 14. I hope that is ok.

I am glad that you like the stuff about relationality and mutuality – it really excites me. I am sure that this is at the heart of what Paul is saying, not only about male / female relationships, but also arising from the relationship of the Trinity. However, when you use the language of submission in the Trinity, you are in danger of creating what is effectively a **subordinationist** relationship between the Father and the Son, and I am very nervous about this. This is key for our text. If we don't establish what we mean by the language of submission, then we muddy the waters and introduce elements into the text which are not there.

I would really like you to unpack what you mean by 'submission' within the context of the Trinity. Do you mean that A has a will separate from B and is able to contradict B, but follow B's will out of submission? After all, this is what one means when one talks about submission between a man and a woman, a husband and a wife. However, when applied to the Trinity it would have significant implications about the unity of the Trinity.

You ask about the 'body language' and how that is used. I agree with you that it varies, but I do not think that it is quite as stark as you portray it, perhaps Paul is subtler in his use of language than we give him credit for. So when he uses the language of the body in relation to the Lord's Supper in 1 Corinthians 11:17–34, he is indeed speaking about the bread and the wine, 'reminding us of Christ's body and his sacrifice', but he is also doing much more than that – as indeed Jesus himself was doing when he chose to share one loaf of bread and one cup among his disciples.

Paul is writing about the Lord's Supper in the context of a discussion about caring for one another, about maintaining order in worship and of recognizing the Body of Christ – hence the direction the discussion takes in chapter 12. That is why he asks the question: 'Or do you despise the church of God and humiliate those who have nothing?' (1 Corinthians 11:22). One might even suggest that his warning after his description of the institution of the Lord's Supper is the corollary of this: 'For those who eat and drink without recognising the body of the Lord eat and drink judgement on themselves' (1 Corinthians 11:29).

I am sure that 'body' here has a dual meaning – that it is meant to refer not only to the physical representation in the bread but also to the people of God, the body of Christ. It is interesting that here alone in the passage Paul refers to the body without the blood; everywhere else they are always referred to together, except in the **Words of Institution**. This being the case, we need to take Paul's body language and imagery very seriously indeed as the defining metaphor for this section and as a key tool for understanding his writing about church order and men and women.

So we move on to the rest of our passage. Paul uses the language of head (*kephalē*) constantly here. He has established the mutuality of man/woman, reflecting the mutuality of the Trinity and of Christ as the head of the body, and so he now goes on to spell out what this interdependence means for their behaviour in worship and for order in the church. In the preceding section Paul has been clear that our interdependence means that, although we may be free in Christ, we have significant responsibilities towards one another: 'I am not seeking my own good but the good of many, so that they may be saved' (1 Corinthians 10:33). These responsibilities will fundamentally affect the way we behave towards one another, and the way we order our worship; hence the flow of his argument into this next section.

Paul moves on to talk about something practical – clothing in worship for both men and women. This is based on an acknowledgment of who we are before God, and therefore in relation to one another. He first addresses the men, and then moves on to the women. Paul requires that a man should never pray or prophesy with his head covered, otherwise he will dishonour his head. Here he uses *kephalē*, the same word he used in the previous verse to speak of Christ in relation to man, so we need to ask whether Paul is speaking here about the man's physical head or his metaphorical head. And does it change? Clearly the issue of dis/honour really matters: it is woven throughout the whole passage and is behind much of the argument. I am not at all clear where you find the basis for your argument that 'Paul then goes on to say that man is not to be subject to any creature, and a covered head is a sign of subjection.' I just cannot see that in the text, as it does not speak about his relationship with other creatures or use the language of subjection.

The woman's head is dishonoured if it is uncovered when she prays and prophesies. It is not that she should not be praying and prophesying in public worship; on the contrary, it is quite clear that she should be. But, as with the men, we need to question whether she is behaving in a manner that inappropriately expresses her freedom such that others are offended or shamed, and maybe even caused to sin. We can read of the **Dionysiac** celebrations held at that time in Corinth, where men and women would exchange their clothes as a ritual act. Paul's call to both men and women is thus to remember their gender, and not to distort the glory of creation seen in maleness and femaleness.

This subject of women covering their heads, along with other issues, was very particular to the time, as is evident by how few women today follow this particular injunction. I am guessing that you don't? While it is not clear whether Paul is here speaking about a woman wearing a veil or binding back her hair when she prays or prophesies, it seems that in this society the arrangement and/or covering of a woman's hair were delineators of their own status and respectability and of that of their families. If a woman were to be unveiled in the street in Jewish circles, it could lead to divorce – the shame was considered so great.

It is therefore hardly surprising that if women were exercising their new-found freedom by standing up and leading the people in worship through prayer and prophecy with no head covering, this would cause a stir or even a scandal. It may have been the cause of societal shame to their families, and of impure and inappropriate thoughts among the men present. Therefore, women and men alike should not stand on their rights to be free, but instead should think of the needs of others and not seek 'their own good but the good of many'. The aim here is to preserve the freedom of the women to pray and prophesy, but in a truly Christian context and in a *culturally* appropriate way, as is demonstrated by the fact that hardly anyone would expect a woman to cover her head today, but neither would we want women – or men – to behave in a way which gave offence or brought the gospel into disrepute. I suppose it is a bit like the discussion we had once at college about the way some of our students were dressing. Some of the younger female students were wearing low-slung jeans and revealing tops. On one level they were dressing no differently from their non-Christian friends, so they were culturally appropriate, but we had to question whether a different standard is required of Christians.

However, Paul's injunction has another reason behind it, which is to do with the language of glory. Glory is a wonderful word in Scripture: it is a term used to manifest God's power and his attributes. Thus, in verse 7 when Paul speaks of man as the image and glory of God, he is stating that man is the culmination of creation. He is not implying that woman is not created in the image of God – indeed nothing would have been further from his mind. By going on to speak of woman as the glory of man, he immediately evokes just that. She is the one in whom man rejoices, who manifests his power and attributes most fully: 'This at last is bone of my bones and flesh of my flesh' (Genesis 2:23 ESV) – one flesh, one body, and therefore demonstrated to be also in the image of God. She is made from man and indeed 'for the sake of man' (11:9, my translation, picking up on the repetition of the preposition *dia*). Paul uses exactly the same language of Christ in 2 Corinthians 8:9. He writes, 'For you know the grace of our Lord Jesus Christ, that though he was rich, yet for your sake he became poor, so that you through his poverty might become rich', which clearly points to the mutuality which Paul intends in this passage. Adam was the one who needed help and was incomplete on his own. So God gave him the woman, who was his glory, to minister to him, to be his helper, 'for his sake'.

The women thus take authority on their heads – presumably by covering them – as a sign to the angels of the churches (as Morna Hooker argues)[8] of the restoration of the created order, so that they can rejoice even as they did at creation. It makes no sense to say that authority here refers to her *husband's* authority over her. If Paul had meant that, he would have surely written that 'the woman ought to have *submission* on her head . . .' (the words 'symbol of' do not appear in the Greek and have been inserted by translators in order to try to make sense of the verse). This is a sign that women do have the authority to speak and to minister.

Paul goes on to explain this even more clearly in what are some of the most remarkable verses about the mutuality of men and women, reflecting what he has said about the mutuality within the marriage relationship in 1 Corinthians 7:1–5. Men and women belong to one another, he says in verse 11: neither is independent of the other, and one cannot exist without the other. Although woman may have come from man in the first place, now man comes from woman. As has been pointed out by several commentators, this even applies to Jesus, who came from a woman,[9] from Mary, as we assert regularly in our creeds.

This mutual dependency is the climax and the key to Paul's argument, and it is rounded off by his assertion that all come from God. This throws us right back to the beginning of the argument: all belong together, and no one should do anything to hurt another – an interdependency and mutuality that frees the other and reflects the Trinity. Paul then sums it up once more with a practical and clear call for the difference between the sexes to be preserved (11:13–14).

In many ways the issue of head covering is particular to the time, but the principles remain the same. What Paul is dealing with here, and throughout the letter, is how we are to behave as a Christian community, and how we should behave as men and women within that community. The key thing to take from this passage is the importance of gender differences and how we honour one another within the kingdom of God.

This is why I think that 1 Corinthians 14:33ff. speaks of submission. It seems that the women were probably chattering loudly. *Lalein*, used here by Paul for 'speak', is not the usual word. It is quite a derogatory term which is often used to denote sound with no meaning. Indeed, it is used at about the same time by Plutarch to say that dogs and apes could *lalein*, but they could not speak rationally. Clearly we don't know the context, but it could well be that women were disrupting the worship. They may well have been sitting separately from the men as in a traditional synagogue. There would have been a great temptation to chatter about what was going on, but Paul says this is not acceptable and they should be silent.

In other words, the women need to submit their own needs to the needs of the community and if they have questions, they should ask their husbands when they get home. This is entirely reasonable and in fact gives permission for women to be taught and to learn, something which we will find again in 1 Timothy 2. Paul is not saying that women should not prophesy and pray, or be involved in ministry. Indeed, up until now Paul has constantly used the inclusive word *adelphoi*, meaning 'brothers and sisters', when speaking about ordering church worship. I think that to suggest that he is concerned with ultimate authority and weighing up prophecies is to bring our own issues to the text rather than Paul's. I am not sure that Paul was interested in 'ultimate authority', unless we are talking about Christ, and even then his language constantly returns to that of the servant.

Anyway, I am aware that this has been a mammoth offering. I feel I have had to cover a lot of ground so that we can move on to Ephesians, but it was a lot of work! I have to say, the more I study this subject, the more I love Paul and his theology of grace!

I trust that all have returned to school ok and that you are getting back into a routine at work.

With love in Christ
Lis

From:	**Clare Hendry**
To:	Lis Goddard
Subject:	Deep breath

Dear Lis
Thank you so much for your latest – certainly much food for thought. I had hoped to get something off to you last week, but with the start-up of lots of things at church and my stepfather's funeral last Friday, it was rather a packed week.

There is so much that I could discuss further, but I will restrict myself to clarifying a few points.

In commenting on working under various male 'bosses', I certainly wasn't trying to use it as an argument for male headship. It was merely a reflection on my experience. I totally agree with you that the key question is not whether men or women can live up to the call of leadership, but what scripturally is their calling under God.

I do want to go back to your example of women leading a local church on their own. You give Phoebe, Lydia and Nympha as examples of women mentioned alone without husbands. I'll agree with you that they are there in Scripture without a husband in sight! However I really have to challenge your proposing them as examples of women clearly leading local churches, examples, which I said I would love to look at if they were there. I went back to the books, starting with the Bible and I cannot see clear evidence at all that these women were such leaders. Phoebe in Romans 16 is called a servant/deaconess and has been of great help to Paul but there is no clear evidence that she was the main leader of the church in Cenchrea. The text just doesn't give us evidence either way.

On to Lydia in Acts 14. She is clearly an important woman and opens up her house to Paul twice and it becomes the centre of Christian worship in that area. But again there is no clear evidence, either way, whether she was the head of that local church.

Finally Nympha in Colossians 4 – a more interesting lady or was she? There is some debate over whether Nympha was male or female. The transliterated Greek name may be either male or female depending on the accent. Much depends on the pronoun for house and the Greek manuscripts vary so some have it as 'his', some as 'her' and others as 'their'. I think more manuscripts go with the female reading. But again all we are told is that the church was in her house. Does that mean she has to be the head of that church or that she is a faithful Christian who has a house big enough for the local church to meet in? I am still waiting to be convinced that there is clear textual evidence that women headed up the local church on their own.

Just to clarify what I meant with regard to the Trinity, I do think there is an order in the relationships. I definitely do not hold a subordinationist view, but rather the more widely held view of 'relational subordination'. So I see God the Son and God the Holy Spirit as being subordinate to God the Father, as throughout Scripture we never see them commanding the Father, but rather doing his will. However, and this is important, the Son and Holy Spirit are in no way inferior to the Father in nature or being (in the same way that a woman called to be submissive to her husband is in no way inferior or any less created in the image of God). The Son and Holy Spirit are co-equal and co-eternal with God the Father, because they are of the same substance as the Father.

I agree with what you say concerning head covering: Paul seemed to have no problem with women praying and prophesying in public. However, I don't see how you reach your position on the significance of head covering in those days which, if I read you correctly, is that 'Paul's call to both men and women is thus to remember their gender and not distort the glory of creation . . .' I think the passage deals with much more than this, and while you have gone into great detail on many things, I still don't feel you have fully answered my question about the significance of the order in verse 3. I think that again we will have to agree to disagree.

I have just reread the last couple of pages of your email before you go on to look at chapter 14, and I say 'Amen' to so much, but then we part company. Man was created by God for his pleasure, joy and glory. Likewise woman was created to be the glory of man, finding her fulfilment in being a helper for man. I know that is like a red rag to a bull, but I can't see how else you can explain I Corinthians 11:7, which says 'the woman is the glory of man'. Having read what you have written, I have returned to the commentaries and other books, and I am still convinced by my reading of verse 10.

I think that in some ways we have less to debate on chapter 14, as much of what we have said flows from chapter 11. As our study of 1 Corinthians comes to a close, I feel I have rather short-changed you, but we must leave it there and encourage folk to do further reading for themselves.

I'd better get this off to you before my peace is shattered by the return of Kate and Alistair from school. It has been rather nice to sit down and quietly work on this after a couple of very busy weeks at St James's. Now we need to kick off with Ephesians.

Love in Christ
Clare

To ponder
How do you see this passage fitting within 1 Corinthians as a whole? How do you understand Paul's 'head' language?
How does this relate to our calling to image God as men and women? How will this look in the church?

Pray
Thank God for the freedom to worship.
Ask God to show you how to exercise your gifts and calling in a way that doesn't dishonour him.

7. Who wears the trousers? Exploring Ephesians

Suggested reading: Ephesians 1 – 6

From:	**Clare Hendry**
To:	Lis Goddard
Subject:	Getting to the heart of things

Hi Lis

Sorry for the slight delay in getting started on Ephesians, but the Hendry household has been battling with various illnesses.

Carrying on from our discussion on headship in 1 Corinthians, I wondered what your thoughts on the Ephesians 5:21–33 passage are? For me, this has been one of the most important passages in my thinking on the whole headship/leadership issue. I have always understood that the passage is looking at the role of husband and wife, and linking it to the relationship that Christ has with the church. I am only too aware of the wrong application of this passage, where it has been used by a few men as an excuse for bullying and even abusing their wives. But properly understood in its context, it lays down some important principles for how a husband and wife are to relate to each other.

This passage on husbands and wives flows directly out of the previous verse (5:21), where it says that members of the Christian community should be submissive to one another out of reverence for Christ. I have always understood this to be a key foundation for how we should deal with all fellow-Christians, by putting them first and seeking to minister to them. Paul then goes on to look at specific relationships and how this works out for the husband and wife. The wife is called to submit to her husband as to the Lord, because 'the husband is the head of the wife as Christ is the head of the church, his body, of which he is the Saviour' (Ephesians 5:23b). So the relationship between husband and wife is to reflect the relationship between Christ and the church. As the church is to submit to Christ, so also wives are called to submit to their husbands in everything. This is not easy to do in a Christian marriage, but it raises even more issues for Christian women married to non-Christian husbands. I still think it applies to all Christian wives, whatever their husband's faith, although it does need further explanation and application.

Paul goes on to address the role of the husband. Husbands are called to love their wives as Christ loved the church. I find it amazing that, when people look at this passage, the focus often seems to be on wives being submissive, and it can be presented as wives being downtrodden and treated as second-class citizens. But when you look at what the husbands are called to do, it puts it into perspective. Christ loved the church so much that he gave his life for it. Wow – is that a tough call for husbands! Again we see the reflection of Christ's love for the church in the relationship between husband and wife. It's also important to note that the roles to which husband and wife are called are unconditional. So often in a marriage relationship, even if a couple accept what Paul is laying out here, they agree to do it on condition that the husband/wife fulfils their part. Yet by my reading of these verses, Paul lays down no conditions.

Now I realize that some might agree with my interpretation of this passage, but then say that it applies only to the marriage relationship. However, I can't see any reason for limiting it to headship only in personal relationship in the home. Surely the man is either head of his family and in all areas or he's not. If that is the case, then how does it work in a situation where the woman is 'head' of the local church, for example as a vicar who is married? How can she be head of her husband in the church setting and yet he is head of her in the family situation? What happens if some situation arises which cannot be neatly fitted into the family box or the spiritual box? Not that you can think of life in boxes – all areas of life have a spiritual dimension to them.

I'm going to stop there as I have to dash out, and I want to get this off to you.

Hope you are well and not getting too overwhelmed by work and family. Look forward to seeing you soon.

Clare

From:	**Lis Goddard**
To:	Clare Hendry
Subject:	Submission for all

Dear Clare

Thank you so much for your last email. Like you, I love this passage and think it is key to understanding the marriage relationship.

You are surely right that this passage has wider implications because it is based on Ephesians 5:21. The whole of the teaching on husbands and wives flows from this verse, which is earthed in the preceding passage about holy living and conduct within the church. What is so often lost in our Bibles is that verse 21 is inextricably linked to verse 22, which doesn't even have its own verb, but refers back to the verb of verse 21. Thus, in the original it says, 'Submit to one another out of reverence for Christ, wives to your husbands as to the Lord' (taking here the NIV translation, but without the repetition).

This interests me because it makes wives and husbands dependent on one another. Submission within the body of Christ is not gender specific; it is intended to be universal. Paul then goes on to give us a particular application of how this submission works out in practice, but the application is dependent on, and not divorced from, the submission expected of everyone within the body, 'out of reverence for Christ'. Why would we, male or female, submit to one another 'out of reverence for Christ', other than, in him, counting others better than ourselves and seeing Christ when we see them?

It has long fascinated me that no one would argue, on the basis of this passage, that wives should not love their husbands, despite the fact that it is only husbands who are told to love their wives here. When Jesus says in his final discourse in John 15:12ff., 'My command is this: love each other as I have loved you. Greater love has no-one than this: to lay down one's life for one's friends', we take it as read that this applies to all Christians and not just to men. It would radically change our theology if we were to make that shift. So when we speak of the husband being called to love his wife with the self-giving, sacrificial love of Christ, we are just re-emphasizing something that is true for all Christians. Why are the two general commands applied in this way? And why has the church consistently failed to apply both equally?

There is much more I could say in response to your opener, but that would risk a bit of a ramble, and it would be good perhaps just to start with this.

Hope your family are on the mend. Life here is hectic – I am glad it is nearly my day off!

With love in Christ
Lis

From:	**Clare Hendry**
To:	Lis Goddard
Subject:	Healthy family

Dear Lis

Good to hear back from you. My family now seems all fully recovered. I hope life is slightly less hectic for you.

I see very little in what you said that I wouldn't wholeheartedly agree with. I do think we are all called as Christians to submit to one another, taking Ephesians 5:21 as a kind of heading for the following verses. But I am still not sure that we are called to submit in the same way. If we were, then why does Paul spell out different ways of relating? Surely the verses that follow verse 21 would be redundant if we are just called to submit one to another without any distinction. I think Paul is laying out a clear pattern of how a husband and wife are to relate to each other – a way that shows their **complementarity**. While verse 21 acts as a general title, Paul seems to go on to say that there are distinctive ways in which people are called to relate to one another. If we take the next two pairs Paul mentions – children and parents, slaves and masters – in what way are parents to submit to their children and slave-masters to submit to their slaves, except in love and wanting the best for them?

Your observations on the two commands of submitting to one another and loving one another as Christ loved us (John 15:12) are helpful. I certainly see that all of us, both male and female, are called to love one another and to submit to one another, if you understand submission as putting the other person first by seeking to minister to them. However, I still think that we are called to different roles. I'm not sure how what you said necessarily does away with the husband being the head of the wife, as stated in Ephesians 5:23. Headship should certainly be based on the model of Christ.

In preparation for a sermon recently, I spent a lot of time reflecting on what Christ did for us on the cross, and then I thought about what you said in your email. Surely Christ, who clearly is the head of the church (verse 23), showed the greatest submission and love by laying down his life for us. In Luke 22:42 Jesus prays to God: 'Father, if you are willing, take this cup from me; yet not my will, but yours be done.' Christ, who is fully divine and equal with God the Father, submitted to the Father's will. But he had a distinct role in the Trinity, which led him to die on the cross to pay the penalty for our sin. Can the husband not still be the head of the wife as Christ is the head of the church, and in his headship reflect the model of Christ who loves the church and was willing to die for it? Also some of my understanding of headship here in this passage flows out of my interpretation of the relationship first established in creation, as we discussed in the chapter on Genesis. Interestingly, every passage that deals with the marriage relationship states that the wife should submit to her husband, and uses the same verb (*hypotassō*, 'submission'), which is a voluntary, loving act.

How do you understand Ephesians 5:23 and Paul's use of the term 'head' for the husband? I know we want to focus on the role of women in ministry in this book, but much of my understanding of the issues comes from this passage. As I said in my last email, I can't imagine how I could be head of the local church (i.e. vicar) if I were to take this passage to mean that my husband is head over me as his wife, and I should therefore submit to him.

I guess it comes down to understanding the place of verse 21, and there seems to be three ways of looking at it:

The verb for submission here does not call for mutual submission in the relationships that Paul outlines (James Hurley takes this approach).[1]

1. Mutual submission is required, in that we are all called to submit to one another and to love one another, but there is a distinction in how that is worked out between the husband and wife.
2. Mutual submission is required, but with no distinctive application between the genders.

I hope I'm not going round in circles! I look forward to hearing your thoughts on this.

Love
Clare

From:	**Lis Goddard**
To:	Clare Hendry
Subject:	More than words

Dear Clare

Thanks so much for your email. Our family have been in the wars rather with various coughs and colds and then, as you clearly learned from my auto-reply, I managed to come off my bike and break my collar bone – the pedal snapped off rather dramatically and I flew over the top of the bike! It's taken rather a long time to recover, but I have been thoroughly spoilt by great children, husband and friends, who have really helped out when I was good for nothing.

I will respond to your points in order, if I may? You are right that there is a difference between the three pairs of relationships to which Paul refers. Clearly the relationships between slaves and masters and parents and children are not the same as between husbands and wives. Slaves and children are told to 'obey' their masters and parents respectively, a verb that is not used of wives. Indeed, I would contend that there is a significant difference in meaning between 'submit' and 'obey' and, despite the usage in the Book of Common Prayer, it is interesting that the verb 'obey' is not in fact applied to the wife/husband relationship here, although Paul could easily have used it.

As I understand it, this is because there is a crucial difference between these two verbs. Obedience, as used here, can be demanded and indeed required; it is the inevitable response of a weaker party in a power relationship. Submission is qualitatively different. In the sense it is used both of Christ and of us, his body, submission is the free self-giving of one's will and being to the other, or as you so beautifully put it, 'a voluntary, loving act'. I disagree with James Hurley, because I believe that *all* Christians are commanded throughout the New Testament to live in this self-giving, servant way towards one another (see e.g. Philippians 2:1–11).

I really loved your beautiful description of Christ's submission and sacrifice. And yet I also wanted to say a big 'but'. It was indeed the Son who was called to 'empty himself and . . . [become] obedient even unto death' (Philippians 2:7–8 RSV), but the truth is also that the whole Trinity was involved in that very act of redemption. Surely this is vital for our understanding of the interrelation of the Trinity. I noticed that you were rightly very careful to say, 'Surely Christ, who clearly is the head of the church (verse 23) showed the greatest submission and love by laying down his life for us . . . Christ who is fully divine and equal with God the Father submitted to the Father's will.' That is absolutely fine, but you then make the leap to headship, by assuming that because *Jesus* submitted to his Father, the eternal Son remaining fully divine and equal with God the Father, wives should submit to their husbands, with all the implications of human power and authority of the non-biblical word 'headship'.

You said in your final email on 1 Corinthians, 'I see God the Son and God the Holy Spirit as being subordinate to God the Father, as throughout Scripture we never see them commanding the Father, but rather doing his will.' I want to ask you whether we can really divide the will of the **triune** God in this way? Are you suggesting that the Son and the Spirit are subordinating their wills to that of God the Father, that they have a separate, different will that they need to subjugate in order to be commanded by his will? Otherwise, it is surely meaningless to say that they do the will of the Father, when in essence it is the expression of their corporate triune will. This would make it irrelevant to the relationship between men and women, because here we are definitely dealing with two separate wills.

I find it very interesting that from this passage you draw teaching *on the roles* for husbands and wives. I suppose this is partly because we understand the term 'head' in such different ways. As I explained when we looked at 1 Corinthians 11, I am convinced that Paul intended 'head' to mean just that – 'head', and here in verse 23 there is a clear example of it being immediately juxtaposed with body language. If the meaning of head was expected to conjure up for us a physical picture, an integrated, totally interdependent organic being, then this is not about roles, but about relationship – about how we relate to one another, how we are dependent upon one another.

I do not infer from this that men and women/wives and husbands are indistinguishable – a criticism often thrown at those who take my position. On the contrary, I am very clear that there are, and must be, very real differences between us, as I indicated when discussing Genesis and the image of God language. However, I am also clear that the differences are not, biblically, of role (except biologically).

I don't think that there is space here to explore those differences in detail. Suffice it to say, I think that the reasons for Paul being specific in his application of the two general commands to the different sexes may have something to do with our temptations to prevailing sins within the marriage relationship. So, for example, I believe that women are often tempted to independence, wanting to run things their own way, to the point where they exclude, alienate or nag men, whereas men can often be guilty of objectify-ing women in a lustful way, rather than loving and valuing them in the way that God intended.

I hope this is helpful and that you are keeping well. I guess, like us, you are teetering on the edge of a new term.

With so much love in our Lord
Lis

From:	**Clare Hendry**
To:	Lis Goddard
Subject:	Final thoughts

Dear Lis
How's the shoulder doing? I hope it is nearly back to full mobility and not giving you any more pain. When something like that

happens, we realize how much we rely on having fit and healthy bodies, especially when trying to look after a family as well as everything else we're doing. I'm glad to hear that your family are now fit and well again.

Sorry, this is about a week later than I said. I am still working through a pile of marking and seem to have a lot of talks to prepare. Roll on the holidays! I imagine that you are equally busy with the end of term looming.

It just happened that one of the talks I was doing this week was on Ephesians 5, so I was able to go over the passage again and do a little more reading from the commentaries. I also recently had one those rare occasions of being alone in the car for an hour or so, and I spent a lot of that time thinking about the passage and how it relates not just to the marriage relationship but also to women and ministry.

I agree with your thoughts on the difference between 'obey' and 'submit'. I was looking at the passage last night with a group of married couples. I was trying to emphasize that the submission is 'as to the Lord'. In other words, it should be done willingly and as a way of honouring and serving God in marriage. But I do think that Paul is dealing with roles and order, which flows from Genesis and the creation story. I know we see this differently. But it can be argued that there was male headship and authority from the very beginning. As I've said, what the Fall did was to bring in an abuse of that headship for some couples. You refer to our discussion of 1 Corinthians 11, with 'head' meaning just that, and so you give a picture of an integrated, interdependent, organic being, and then you go on to say that this is not about roles, but about relationship – how we relate to one another and are dependent on one another. I don't see those last two points necessarily being opposed to a headship type of reading. Surely one would say that it is about how a wife and husband relate to one another, and there is obviously a dependent relationship, as we see back in Genesis which speaks about the man leaving his mother and father, and the couple becoming one flesh. Yet there is an order in the relationship that seems to be present in this passage in Ephesians as well as in other passages.

We are in total agreement about the fact that God created man and woman to be different. You have always maintained this from your **egalitarian** viewpoint. It must be frustrating when people try to put words into the mouths of folk holding your position. I guess it happens both ways. I really wish that people would actually ask where we are coming from, rather than just assume (i) that they fully know what we believe, and (ii) that everyone in either the egalitarian or the **complementarian** group holds exactly the same views. When talking to friends who share my complementarian perspective, I certainly find that we can vary on many things within that position.

I think we are probably coming towards the end of anything further we can say on this subject. It would be good to explore how we apply these Bible passages to our lives, especially with regard to our ministry. For me, the most obvious application is to my marriage, rather than to my ministry but, as I've explained, I do think it has implications for the position of a woman in ministry too.

When people think about the man as the head of the family, they often imagine an abuse of power, but when you see a man exercising biblical headship in a godly way, it works so well and is great to experience. In our own marriage, when Steve and I don't agree on something, we normally pray through things to seek God's guidance and thereby come to some compromise. I can think of only one situation when we really reached stalemate, and that was over whether we should baptize our children. Steve is from a background that doesn't believe in infant baptism, whereas my understanding of covenantal theology has led me to believe that in Christian families you should baptize children. Compromise wasn't quite possible, as baptizing only half the child wasn't an option! So we had them dedicated instead, and Steve did have the final decision.

I am all for women being involved in church leadership; I think the church would be a much poorer place without them. I work in a church where both men and women are on the leadership team, which I think reflects a biblical picture of ministry and is very healthy. But the head of that church is ultimately the vicar (a man), so I guess, in more worldly language, the buck stops with him. Now the leadership/headship exercised by him is not domineering, and he certainly appreciates women's input in leading the church and in the many roles they fulfil. I have always found my bosses who held complementarian views like mine to be very supportive of my role, including my preaching and teaching ministry.

Well I had better finish – the marking and washing await. I am looking forward to the AWESOME conference. Maybe we can grab a few moments there to talk further about how things are going with this book.

With love in Christ
Clare

From:	**Lis Goddard**
To:	Clare Hendry
Subject:	The last word

Dear Clare
Thank you for your thoughtful email – it was great to hear from you again. A lot has happened in the Goddard household since I last wrote.

The shoulder still aches, but is now pretty much in full working order after lots of swimming and tennis. Jono has managed to break his wrist – cycling with his hands crossed: apparently 'it doesn't work'! It was a rather nasty accident which necessitated a midnight operation – all fun and games.

Incidentally, it was interesting that you referred to me as an 'egalitarian', as that is not a term I generally use of myself. Egalitarians often do not acknowledge that there is a difference between the sexes, and I certainly do and would want to celebrate it.

However, I do not think it is role or power based, which is a key difference between us.

It is fascinating to me how often we keep returning to Genesis and our understanding of that passage. As you know, we find ourselves in disagreement over whether male headship is a **creation ordinance** or not, and that really is a crux issue in this whole debate, isn't it? This seems to hinge on several things, and one is this: we both hold that redemption restores creation order and reverses the ravages of the Fall, but we fundamentally disagree on what that means. When 'a man leaves his father and mother', you read into that a 'dependent relationship', whereas I would read an interdependent relationship (thus Ephesians 5). This quite clearly changes the way marriage works and the way I anticipate relationships between men and women to work generally.

Andrew and I have always operated on the basis that we put each other first in all things, that under God our primary calling is to love each other and to serve each other by looking for the other's good before our own: a sort of trinitarian love model 'within the love of God: Father, Son, and Holy Spirit' to quote the marriage service. If you are both operating with this premise and each trusts the other entirely, then it makes for an incredibly open relationship, which frees the other to be themselves. There's never been a situation where we have been unable to make a decision and had to defer to one or the other. We have spent most of our working life job-sharing, boxing and coxing our professional lives and our parenting, not because of issues of headship, but because we wanted to parent our children together, and didn't want that to be just me. Andrew wanted to be involved too.

Clearly our understanding of Ephesians 5 doesn't preclude a woman from being responsible for a worshipping community. I have been. To be honest, I feel it is healthier for such a community to have both male and female leadership – both male and female are made in the image of God, and a church may thrive with either a man or woman as 'the' leader.

The whole question of marriage and Ephesians 5 is interesting, particularly when one is aware of the harm that is done by *both* sides of the debate through more extreme teaching, which can lead to dysfunctional marriages in a variety of ways.

Dear Clare, thank you for bearing with me through the catalogue of Goddard family disasters! I shall try to be less accident-prone for the next chapters. I am looking forward to tackling 1 Timothy next – one of my favourite parts of Scripture.

With love and best wishes in Christ
Lis

To ponder
How do you relate Paul's injunction to all his readers to 'submit to one another out of reverence to Christ' with that to wives?
Why do you think Paul gives different instructions to wives and husbands? What should this look like in practice?
How do you think this should affect women's roles within the church (if at all)?

Pray
Thank God for the examples of self-giving, Christ-like marriages which you have been privileged to see. What are the characteristics of these marriages that have impressed you?
Pray for your own marriage / relationship or the marriages of your friends, that God's love may be what defines them.

8. Silence is golden?
   ## What 1 Timothy 2 tells us

Suggested reading: 1 Timothy 2

From:	**Lis Goddard**
To:	Clare Hendry
Subject:	Once more into the breach

Dear Clare

It was great to see you at the conference. It was, as ever, really busy, and it was good to see so many women there, all of whom God is using in ministry in one way or another. Isn't it amazing that there are women all over the country just getting on with living out their calling, growing churches, preaching the gospel and often working in some really tough contexts. I love the fact that we can give each other support and encouragement.

But on to 1 Timothy, particularly 1 Timothy 2. I have to say that I love this passage, which is rather unfashionable among many women. I have always seen it as a liberating passage. Perhaps this has to do with having a remarkable mother, who taught me to see what was going on in Scripture, to understand it within its context, and to allow it to speak to me in mine. I can still remember her helping me when I was quite young and first discovered this passage. I got quite frustrated by it – even then I didn't like to be quiet – and she told me that I had to think about the parts of the world where women were not allowed to learn or to go to school. I remember looking with her at those places, such as Afghanistan today, where women and girls were totally untaught. Then she asked me to imagine what it would feel like to hear Paul's words if I were one of those girls or women. A light came on then which has never gone out. I suddenly understood that Paul was saying something positive, not something negative, and I understood this was because I had been enabled to take off my mufflers and had begun to hear him as he was speaking to his original audience.

Paul was saying that women should *learn*! This was revelatory and remarkable. This amazing injunction is Paul's response to a very difficult situation where false doctrine was being put forward by those who were untaught and who, it would appear, were usurping power inappropriately. I'm sure that we will not disagree on this starting point: it isn't very controversial.

The key questions for me are *how* and *why* should women learn? First of all *how*? We are told they should learn in quietness and with full submission. Traditionally this has been taken to mean that women must not speak and must be submissive to men. However, I am not convinced that this is a fair reading of this verse. The word for quietness has been used before in the passage at 2:2, where Paul has encouraged prayer for kings and all those in positions of power, 'that we may lead peaceful and quiet lives in all godliness and holiness'. So the implication is not that they should remain totally silent, as several translations would have it, but that they should learn with a quiet and God-centred demeanour. This is reinforced by the language of full submission.

The assumption that this refers to the relationship between men and women is, I think, built upon a certain reading of what follows with regard to Adam and Eve. However, the text does not say to whom the woman should submit, and it certainly does not say that it should be to men. Indeed, it makes much more sense within the flow of the passage as a whole for the submission to be to God. In the previous verse Paul has just said that the appropriate attitude for women is 'God-reverence' (a literal translation of the Greek word which our Bibles translate as 'godliness'), and therefore it makes absolute sense within this context for the submission to refer to God.

Of course, the other reason suggested for applying the sub-mission to the male-female relationship is Paul's use of the language of authority, when he writes, 'I do not permit a woman to teach or to assume authority over a man; she must be quiet' (1 Timothy 2:12 ESV). In order to unpack this, I suppose we need to look at a bit of the background to what was going on in Ephesus, and why Paul was writing this letter to Timothy while he was there.

The major cult in Ephesus at this time was that of Artemis, the Roman Diana. Her temple was massive and dominated the skyline; it was one of the wonders of the world. All her priests were virgins, who shared leadership with men only if they were castrated – they dominated the men. One of the key points of concern that Paul is addressing in 1 Timothy is the teaching of false doctrine. He begins his injunctions to Timothy with the instruction to 'stay there in Ephesus so that you may command certain people not to teach false doctrines any longer or to devote themselves to myths' (1 Timothy 1:3–4).

Things must have been pretty grim at Ephesus, given that Timothy wanted to leave. We do not know in detail what was happening in the church at Ephesus, but there was clearly a problem with false teaching and this had affected the women. Two thirds of the letter is devoted to the combined weight of false teaching and women. Whether the untaught women were aping the dominant cult or had come under the influence of the 'New Roman woman', the ladette of the ancient world, they were usurping the position of those who held appropriate authority and they were spreading wrong doctrine.

This seems particularly likely given Paul's comment in 1 Timothy 5:15: 'Some have in fact already turned away to follow Satan.' Within the letter there is a range of references with instructions on how women were to behave, such as their conduct in worship (2:10–15), the qualifications for female deacons (3:11), appropriate pastoral behaviour of female elders (5:2), and how to correct younger widows and support older widows (5:3–10, 16). There was clearly a problem, and these women needed to be sorted out.

This would explain why Paul chooses to use such an unusual word in verse 12, when he says that he does not permit a woman to 'exercise authority over a man'. He uses a very strong word, which is rare and is not his usual word for authority. It appears only here in the New Testament and can be used elsewhere to denote the life and death power of a ruler over his people. It can also be translated as 'to commit murder' or 'to assert absolute sway', which is why the King James Version translated it as 'to usurp authority'. It has the connotations of violent overthrow, of someone taking authority that is not rightfully theirs.

This being the case, it seems entirely reasonable for Paul to say that he does not permit a woman to violently seize authority which isn't hers, or, within that context, to teach, particularly if it means that she is teaching false and misleading doctrine. None of us would want that with either men or women. Paul, who has already established elsewhere the principle that women should teach and prophesy, is now helping Timothy to get back to basics, so that those who do teach should themselves be properly taught in a society where things have gone drastically wrong.

He wants women to be taught and equipped, and we see later in the letter that he expects them to be part of church leadership, as we have seen elsewhere in the New Testament. His prohibition on teaching here is firmly linked to their inappropriate grabbing of power. This teaches once again about right relationships within the Christian community: hence the fact that it begins in verse 8 with a command that men should pray 'without anger or disputing' ('quarrelling' in ESV). It is a passage about equipping the people of God to be different, to be salt and light in an alien world. So it really is a very exciting and liberating passage for women!

I am going to stop there. As I have written this, I have been struck by the parallels with our current situation. There are frequent complaints that women are poor preachers and teachers (I'm sure some are – so are some men!), but it is so often because those who preach and teach have not been taught. It is easy in our culture to get a platform because of who you are (or who you are married to), rather than because you have been called, trained and had your calling confirmed. There is something wrong about a situation where a woman has power by default, as so often happens in some of our churches. It disempowers other women and undermines good practice.

Anyway, enough of that. It would be good to hear your thoughts on all of this.

With much love as ever
Lis

From:	**Clare Hendry**
To:	Lis Goddard
Subject:	Counterculture

Dear Lis

I am impressed at such a quick turn round when you have been so busy with the AWESOME conference.

It was really encouraging and interesting to meet so many women in ministry, to hear a little of where they were coming from and what they were up to, although some comments I heard made me realize how much this book is needed. Some folk seemed to be totally unaware that there are other views on headship held by 'sane and normal' people, and that for some groups this is not the minority view. What I appreciate about AWESOME is the desire to bring together all evangelical, ordained, female clergy (what a mouthful!). It is important that women who have a high view of the Bible can take the view that I and others hold about male headship, and that this is a legitimate position. But I didn't always get that impression from some of the folk at the conference.

On to 1 Timothy 2 which, as a preacher to mixed congregations, presents me with some challenges. It is how we apply such teaching (along with other passages) that sometimes divides those that would share my overall view regarding male headship. As I have mentioned, when I was at Oak Hill the majority of students attended chapel when I was preaching, but there were one or two who wouldn't because they felt categorically that women should never teach men. I'll come back later in another email on how I apply this passage.

You have helpfully looked at a lot of the background to this book, so I won't go over that ground, except to pick up on where we disagree. I think it is interesting that Paul in his instructions on worship tells men that they should lift up holy hands in prayer without anger or disputing, and then tells women to dress modestly. I am sure Paul would say that women should also not be angry or involved in disputes, and that men should dress appropriately, but it seems that these issues were problems for different groups of people, and so Paul was speaking into the contemporary situation. There also seems to be a problem, as you say, concerning how women should learn. I am more than happy to say women should learn, but I think you are missing the point of the passage by focusing on the cults that were around and the situation at the time. Surely we can draw principles from such teaching that are applicable today.

I found John Stott's commentary on 1 Timothy and Titus[1] really helpful. He lays down two hermeneutical principles which are important when seeking to understand a biblical passage and to apply it to today's situations. The first is the 'principle of harmony'. The Bible is the Word of God, and God does not contradict himself. So, when interpreting a passage, it is important that you see it in light of the whole of Scripture, as there is consistency in the Bible. The second is the 'principle of history'. When God speaks through the Bible, he does so into a particular time and culture. The Bible contains eternal truth which is universal and **normative**, but its cultural presentation is local and changeable. The challenge is to be able to distinguish between the two and decide what teaching is universal, normative and applicable to today and what is cultural and so not relevant to our day.

Stott goes on to highlight two traps into which we can fall. The first is, as Stott says, to 'enthrone the cultural form': in other words, to give the cultural expression the same standing or authority as the truth or principle that it expresses. For instance, in 1 Timothy 2:8, where it says men must always lift up their hands when they pray, is that a principle of eternal significance to be applied today, or is it a cultural expression of a principle? Some who 'enthrone the cultural form' would argue that men should indeed lift up their hands when praying. They want everything to apply today.

The second trap is where people similarly fail to distinguish between eternal truth and its cultural expression, and so tend to dismiss everything, including the eternal truths – thereby throwing the baby out with the bathwater. So we are left with little to apply, and much of the Bible is regarded as of only cultural relevance.

In his footnote to this passage, Stott critiques the hermeneutics of such authors as Gordon Fee, who conclude that Paul is here addressing a particular situation in Ephesus, which is of cultural relevance rather than of eternal significance, and so Paul's teaching about women in this passage is not thought to be applicable today. My summary of the position (I am sure Stott and Fee would state their positions more eloquently) is that 'I do not permit . . .' cannot, as some would argue, be seen merely as referring to a specific situation in Ephesus rather than a universal one. To declare that a passage in the Bible has only local and transient validity, and is not relevant today, can lead to full rejection of apostolic teaching. After all, isn't much of New Testament teaching addressed to specific situations in the early church, and yet we draw general principles from it?

Again, I have found Stott to be very helpful in suggesting a way forward, which he calls 'cultural transposition'. Rather than try to explain it fully here, I suggest that folk read the relevant section in his commentary. In this passage we need to distinguish between the principle and the cultural outworking of the principle. So we can conclude that men's prayers are to be holy and in the spirit of love, not angry or arguing – this is the general principle. How men are to pray with regard to posture may vary according to culture. For some it will be sitting, others standing or kneeling, and so on. That reminded me of the American students who came from Concordia colleges (Lutheran Missouri Synod) to spend a semester at Oak Hill. When they took a chapel service, we would sit to sing and stand to pray. Scripture calls us to sing before the Lord, but what posture we take will vary according to the prevailing culture / tradition. Moving on to women in worship, the principle is that they are to clothe themselves modestly, with decency, propriety and good deeds, and that is as relevant for women today as it was then. But again, the braided hair, gold, pearls or expensive clothes may vary according to culture. We need to consider what message those things gave out in Paul's day and then think of what the equivalent would be today. If we were to apply that verse literally, I think quite a few women ministers would be failing here, including me, as I think I have appeared up front in pearls!

So what are we to make of the verses that follow? In verses 11 and 12 we have a set of complementary instructions: a woman should learn in quietness and full submission; and then a negative – a woman should not teach or have authority over a man. Does submission always have to be expressed in silence, and equally does 'not exercising authority' always have to be expressed in 'not teaching'? If I thought that to be the case, as do some of my group, then I would not preach to a mixed congregation. However, I am also not sure whether Paul was forbidding these women from teaching because they were ignorant and untaught, or stating that they should not teach at all.

After all, ignorant women holding false doctrine should not be teaching women either, but here Paul only forbids them from teaching men. In line with the **hermeneutic** that I have been using, I would say that it was normative for a woman to submit to a man, and I think it is quite in order to say that, in this context, submission is to men. You also say that Paul has elsewhere established that women can teach and prophesy. I agree up to a point, but if by that you mean that Paul has already established that women can lead a church, then I don't believe that has been proven.

Anyway, it is getting late and my brain is getting addled, so I am off to bed and will finish this off tomorrow . . .

. . . and back again! An early morning swim and a cup of coffee have kick-started my brain into gear. Just a few further thoughts and then I'll hand back to you.

You guessed correctly that I would pick up on the Genesis reference – it is key to understanding why Paul says what he does. Paul is already countercultural to some extent in encouraging all women to learn, He doesn't seem to indicate that the reason for not allowing a woman to teach or exercise authority over a man is because of a lack of education. After all, some women in Ephesus were educated, such as Priscilla who, with her husband Aquila, taught Apollos. I think the basis for why women should not teach men or exercise authority over them is because to do so would violate God's intention in creation. Paul makes two points from the Genesis passage. First in verse 13 he looks at the creation order: Adam was created first, and then Eve was created out of Adam to be a helper. We see the outworking of this, for instance, in the teaching on the roles of husbands and wives in Ephesians. My second point from verse 14 is that it was Eve who failed morally and was deceived. Personally I find this a tough one, but I can't think of another plausible explanation. I look forward to hearing your response on this.

There is obviously more to say on 1 Timothy. One question I have not answered (and it is begging to be asked) is: 'How can I teach a mixed congregation if I believe Paul is saying women should not teach or exercise authority over men? Am I just picking the bits I like and ignoring the rest?' I thought I would leave that until next time.

Hope you are having a good week.

Lots of love
Clare

From:	**Lis Goddard**
To:	Clare Hendry
Subject:	Diving for pearls

Dear Clare

Thank you so much for your last email – sorry for the delay in this one. I have been suffering from a nasty throat infection which has been racing round the family.

I agree with your analysis on the conference. I found myself smiling, because I so often find myself in evangelical groups thinking just the same as you, when I am treated as the one who is completely off the wall and who has lost touch with Scripture. If only as evangelicals we could try to trust one another more, to listen to one another and to work together more, what a difference that would make!

Your response on 1 Timothy sparked off lots of questions for me. You say at the beginning that there are those who would ask why you preach to mixed congregations, given your position on headship. In fact I would go further and ask if this passage is really taken from a creation principle to mean that women cannot teach or have any authority over men, but rather should remain silent, why does this not also apply beyond the church? It seems to me that a creation principle should be all-encompassing, and can't just be made to apply only to discrete areas.

I was surprised that you dismissed the injunction not to dress 'with elaborate hairstyles or gold or pearls or expensive clothes' (1 Timothy 2:9), as surely the point behind this is not only sexual allurement but the re-enforcement of social barriers and differences, both of which are as pertinent today as they have always been. For this reason, I am not entirely sure that Stott's distinctions are helpful. You suggest that being in full submission need not always imply silence, and that 'not exercising authority' need not always be expressed in not teaching, but I just do not see this in the text. If you are going to read the text in this way, I do not see how you can have it both ways.

I wonder why you have not engaged with the meaning of the word *authentein*. It is a key part of this text. You clearly understand it to mean 'the normal functioning authority of a community' whereas to me it appears here to be about *usurping* authority. The whole meaning of the passage depends on how this word is interpreted. Authority is such an important, countercultural concept within the New Testament, and it is one of the reasons why I find the whole idea of male headship completely sub-biblical (i.e. less than the biblical vision).

Jesus is so clear in Mark 10:41–45: 'You know that those who are regarded as rulers of the Gentiles lord it over them, and their high officials exercise authority over them. Not so with you. Instead, whoever wants to become great among you must be your servant, and whoever wants to be first must be slave of all' (vv. 42–44). This has been a recurring theme; authority in the Christian community is not like that found elsewhere – it should not dominate, but it should serve and have a mutuality about it. Therefore, when a group is usurping authority, it presents a major problem that has to be dealt with. Certainly such people should not teach. It is vital that the **Gordian knot** is cut – no wonder that Paul gives such a blanket ban. We know that he does not usually act in this way. It would appear from other passages in 1 Timothy that this referred to a particular group in the Ephesian church. Paul is clearly trying to rectify a difficult situation and to restore order for Timothy.

It is not surprising that Paul goes back to the story of creation and the deception of Eve. First of all, he needs to put the record straight about the Genesis story. The **Gnostics** (whose teaching is clearly a problem in Ephesus) believed that Eve existed before Adam and was the source of all life, doubtless a myth that sat nicely with the Ephesian cult of Artemis, which raised the woman far above the man and did such violence to masculinity. Paul therefore begins by reminding the Ephesians of the depth of their ignorance; Eve could not have given birth to Adam, as he was formed first, then Eve. I hardly need to say that I am not at all convinced that

142 | THE GENDER AGENDA

this is about a hierarchical order in creation: that is not what it says either in Genesis or in this passage. It does not speak about the woman being man's helper or subordinate. The only way one could deduce this is from the violent, abusive language more appropriate to their post-Fall relationship; or from the fact that we are told that Adam was formed first, although we are not told what to deduce from this. In fact it is more clearly linked to the Fall than to anything else, and yet we know that elsewhere Paul attributes the Fall to Adam's weakness (Romans 5:12ff.).

It is probable (although we cannot know for definite) that Paul wrote his first letter to the Corinthians while in Ephesus, and so the epistle may have been known there too. If this were the case, the Ephesians would have been very familiar with the passage in 1 Corinthians 15:42–49 in which Paul very clearly attributes the Fall to Adam: ' . . . in Adam all die' (1 Corinthians 15:22). Given this clear argument in 1 Corinthians, and indeed in Romans, it would hardly be surprising, if those with an anti-male agenda in Ephesus were to use this for their own ends. So Paul is now putting this right.

Paul makes it clear that it was not just the man who fell, the woman did too. Eve was deceived, and here the language is interesting because she is the passive recipient of the deception. The active agent is clearly the serpent, who chooses to deceive the woman. This is of interest within the context of the passage as a whole, because it provides the balancing sentence to the command that women should learn. If women are taught, they will not be so easily deceived. You suggest that in 1 Timothy 2:14 we are presented with a picture of a woman who failed morally and therefore, I assume, needs the authority of man, who didn't fail, to guide her. I know I am **extrapolating** the last part from your argument, but I can't see where else it is going. This makes absolutely no sense to me. There can be no doubt, both from the Genesis account, and from Paul's use of it elsewhere, that both the man and the woman failed, and to concentrate purely upon Eve seems very strange.

Here Paul is focusing upon Eve for a particular reason: he is writing to a context where the world-view is so distorted that women have forgotten the value of men – perhaps some women are at risk of doing this in our society today. He therefore needs to remind women that they too are part of the story of the Fall, and not some Gnostic semi-divine, that they were deceived and that the story of usurping power began with Eve, as she allowed herself to be deceived into believing the serpent's words: 'You will be like God, knowing good and evil' (Genesis 3:5).

The whole point of this section is that Paul is showing that women are fallen, that the nature of that Fall was based on ignorance, and therefore women need to be educated. But he also wants to stress that the Fall and the Gnostic/Ephesian heresy are not the last word for women. This is why he goes on to the amazing verse 15, which has caused commentators so many problems over the years. The literal translation of the Greek is: 'Yet she shall be saved through the childbearing.' My favourite interpretation of this verse, and the one which I think works best, is that Paul is drawing a parallel between Eve and Mary. There is a clear use of the singular here and in the previous verse, which becomes plural at the end of the verse when it speaks about continuing in faith, love and holiness, suggesting that the reference is not to women in general but to a specific woman.[2]

Whereas through one woman's ambition and ignorance the Fall and transgression came, through the other's obedience, submission and knowledge of God came the means of salvation. That is not to say that Mary's act is salvific; salvation is found only through Jesus (1 Timothy 2:5–6). But it is a means by which women are restored from being the agents of the Fall to being agents of the New Covenant. Clearly for women to know salvation for themselves they need to 'continue in faith, love and holiness with propriety'. Understood in this way, the passage as a whole is coherent and works well with the rest of the New Testament's witness regarding women.

Anyway, I think I should stop there. I have given you lots to respond to and I really want to know how you deal with this passage!

With lots of love as ever
Lis

From:	Clare Hendry
To:	Lis Goddard
Subject:	Girl power?

Dear Lis
Wow! Again lots to get my head around.

Regarding Paul's reference to creation, it is inevitable that we will disagree on his use of Genesis, since we disagreed right at the beginning on the application of parts of the creation and Fall stories.

You are absolutely right to pick me up on not engaging with the textual meaning of 'authority' in verse 12. I hadn't done so because, after studying the text, it didn't seem to present a major problem. Indeed, the Greek word for 'authority' is an unusual one, and at first reading may be taken to mean some kind of dominating use of authority. If this were the case, then you might have grounds for understanding it in the way you spelt it out in your last email. However, Craig Blomberg[3] helpfully points towards a study done by Andreas Köstenberger, who maintains that where there are pairs of infinitives, as in verse 12, without exception in the New Testament, they join together either two negative or two positive concepts. Blomberg goes on to quote another study that reinforces this approach. So the only way you can then read 'authority' here with negative connotations is to interpret 'teaching' in a similar way, which does not make sense in this verse.

1 Timothy 2:13–14 is particularly significant in this passage, as here Paul supplies us with the biblical basis for what he has said in the previous verses. Paul looks back to Genesis, to Adam and Eve and to creation. I think Paul's argument for headship does rest on the facts of creation and the Fall, although I know you would not

agree. I am not alone in taking that line. John Stott, in his commentary on 1 Timothy, talks about the origin of headship being in Genesis. If this were not the case, why does Paul refer to it? I can't see an adequate explanation in what you say and I don't agree that this is more about the Fall than about creation. I think it is about both, and I am unable to go along with your line of thought, partly because you base it on a specific understanding of the term 'authority' in verse 12, with which I disagree as already stated.

What Paul actually means about childbirth in verse 15 is a tough one. *Sōthēsetai* ('saved') could mean 'she shall be saved' or 'she shall be kept safe'. I think I am of the same mind as Stott, that it is a reference to Jesus' birth, through which our salvation is achieved. While we shouldn't forget what we owe to Mary, I am not sure that I would say as you do that 'it is a means by which women are restored from being agents of the Fall, to being agents of the New Covenant'. I can't quite see that in Scripture.

You asked me how I came to hold the position I do? From my reading of Scripture and understanding of the teaching as a whole, and not just from 1 Timothy, it is clear that women do teach and that women have sometimes taught men. Some would argue that women such as Priscilla taught alongside her husband and not in a public setting, but surely prophecy is in some way teaching and we certainly see women prophesying in the New Testament.

I think my position is similar to that of Helen Campbell,[4] who speaks on headship, authority and teaching within UCCF. I realize that at one level her position differs from mine, in that she was working in a parachurch organization and I work in the local church. I think that the Bible does only address relationships within the church and home, but there are insights and principles that apply to both situations. Helen states that men and women are equal in nature, and both reflect the image of God, but how they do that within the local church is different and needs to follow creation order, which is also my position.

Helen said that when she was teaching she would make sure that she did less than her male colleagues, and that she would try to make the teaching as interactive as possible, in an attempt to model that authority resides in Scripture rather than in her as the speaker. As I have mentioned, some who hold a similar position to mine on headship would say that any public teaching of men by a woman is in some way exercising headship, so women should only teach other women. While I personally don't agree with that application, I must respect them in the same way that I hope they respect me.

For me, the important link is between headship (having authority) and teaching. While there are clearly strong links between the two, I do not think they are the same activity, so teaching in and of itself does not necessarily mean that you are holding a position of authority. If my occasional preaching at St James's, and the other times when I teach men and women from the Bible, were seen by the congregation as my being the main authoritative person at St James's (i.e. taking a headship position), I would not agree to do it. However, from a human point of view it is clear that Kim, our (male) vicar, is head (boss!) at St James's. So when I teach, I am indeed under the authority of the Word, but I am also accountable in what I am teaching to Kim, the head of this local congregation..

Finally, to pick up on your question on why I apply the headship concept only to the church and home, this is because I can't see any evidence that God is applying it to relationships outside those two spheres. But I do though see where he links what goes on within the household to what is going on in the church, as in 1 Timothy 3.

I am sure there is more to say, but I am running out of steam. Although we are focusing on the differences between our positions, there is actually a lot on which we do agree, even regarding women and ministry!

Whatever you believe about what exactly the Bible teaches about women and ministry, it is clear that women are called to 'ministry' and should be well taught, It makes me cross when women in some churches oversee women's ministry, and yet are not properly equipped to do so, and the church doesn't see the need to train them. Women need theological training just as much as men do!

Good to end with a point on which we do agree. I look forward to hearing back from you. I am now going to make a much-deserved cup of tea and read the Saturday newspaper. During the last few weeks I have been burning the candle at both ends, and sometimes it felt like the middle as well.

I think I told you about a close family friend who died recently. I officiated at the burial. Although I am not sure that was the best situation for my first burial, I certainly would not have refused. It was hard, but I was so glad to be able to perform the service for my friend. Over these last few weeks I have been so aware that, in my weakness, I can rely on God's strength.

With love
Clare

From:	**Lis Goddard**
To:	Clare Hendry
Subject:	Hope for the future

Dearest Clare

It was very good to hear from you again. Thank you for taking the time to write at such a difficult time. It is indeed a privilege to be able to conduct the funerals of those we love, but it can also be heart-rending too. I remember doing the funeral for a dear student whom I had come to know and love very much. She committed suicide soon after I left the college where I was working. It was hard knowing that I had to hold things together for all the others present and so find another time to do my own grieving. I do pray that you have had time to grieve and to do your own remembering, both on your own and with your family. Of course, as Christians one of the wonderful things that transforms our grief is the absolute assurance of resurrection life. I know that you will have held on to this in recent weeks. I will keep praying for you all so much.

Thank you for your response to my screed on 1 Timothy. I just want to pick up on the question that I have flagged up since our Genesis chapter of why this teaching applies only in the church and the family. You say it is because we see it applied only in these spheres in the New Testament, and yet, if it is a creation ordinance, it should surely be universally applicable.

Anyway that is enough. Shall I kick off the concluding chapter? It all seems rather weird to be finishing up – a bit like letting a child loose into the world!

I have a busy time ahead as our church is holding a proper Advent carol service which I am organizing. I am trying to make it accessible for the whole church family. I love Advent as we look forward to our Lord's return and remember that he is the first fruits from the dead.

With so much love
Lis

To ponder

Do you think 1 Timothy was written for a specific situation, and does it have relevance for us today?

How do you make sense of verses 11–15 in the light of the rest of the epistle and of the rest of the New Testament/Bible?

If Paul's injunction not to teach or take authority *is* based on a creation ordinance, how does that relate to life outside the church and family life?

Pray

Thank God for all godly leaders in his church. Name those who have impacted you, and pray for them and their ministry.

Pray for those who are struggling in situations where power is being wielded inappropriately.

9. Conclusion: So what?
Living and relating as the people of God

From:	**Lis Goddard**
To:	Clare Hendry
Subject:	The home straight

Dear Clare

I can't believe that we are embarking on the final chapter of this book: it seems such a long time since we started. We predicted it would be quite a challenge, juggling it with all the other things in our lives, and such a lot has happened in the intervening time. I have moved cities and changed jobs; I have gone from teaching in a theological college to working in a busy parish. It has been a tough time, but I love being back in parish ministry. Our children have grown up and changed in all sorts of ways, and Jonathan is on the verge of leaving home! I guess that by the time the book sees publication the same may be true for Kate and Nell. I wonder what else has changed over the course of writing this book.

Engaging with you on this issue has certainly changed me. I think it has challenged me in all sorts of ways, some that I didn't expect! When I started out, I thought that I had my views on this whole subject all sorted out, but I have discovered all kinds of new things and learned a lot along the way.

I thought, too, that I was pretty untroubled by this whole subject. Yes, it mattered to me to understand Scripture correctly, but if you had convinced me to change my mind, that would have been OK. In fact, as I wrote, I found that this issue matters a great deal to me. I slowly realized that, for me as for you, this issue of women in leadership is not an isolated one: it is tied up with so much else of how I understand the nature and purposes of God as revealed in Scripture. And because of that, it is tied up with how I understand myself in relation to him. This is not just about my calling and whether I am allowed to lead men or not; it is about who I am in Christ. As you can imagine, this clarification has been very important, and writing to you has really brought it into sharper focus.

Linked to that, it has also helped me to concentrate on the biblical, and particularly the New Testament, understanding of authority. I have found myself constantly returning to Mark 10:43 and Jesus' injunction to his disciples that 'it shall not be so among you' (ESV). Indeed, I suppose I have found myself at a bit of a loss to understand how any hierarchy can be imported into a church founded by Christ – but you know that!

One of the things that I have really appreciated has been our friendship, which has developed and deepened. Thank you so much for being such a gracious and patient correspondent. It has seemed absolutely right that at the heart of this dis-cussion about relationship has been a wonderful relationship, and one which God has really blessed. If only the trust and the love that you have shown me as we have grappled with Scripture were evident across the evangelical constituency, as they engage with one another on this issue. So I suppose my prayer is that this book will help others to make the same journey that we have.

I do hope that it has also been a positive experience for you. I know that my family will be pleased when we hand over the manuscript – although Nell can't wait to read the finished article!

Well, I'll send this off to you now and get on with my prepar-ation for a talk for tomorrow morning on 'Learning to hear God'

– should be fun. I plan to have a practical session in there too, so that they get a chance to practise what I preach!

Lots of love in Christ
Lis

From:	**Clare Hendry**
To:	Lis Goddard
Subject:	Straining for the wire

Dear Lis

Are we really on the last chapter?! This book has been with us for such a long time.

I haven't experienced quite as many changes as you have, but as our children are both now in secondary school, we are faced with being parents of teenagers – with the mix of challenges and joys that brings. You were certainly right about the amount of juggling needed, in both the Goddard and Hendry households! Even after this is finished, I am sure that, with the nature of ministry and family life, the juggling will continue.

When we first started, I wondered what would happen if, after looking at all the texts and hearing your side of things, I suddenly saw that you were right and I was wrong. I have found it really valuable to go back to passages and re-examine them. It's also been great to look at other parts of Scripture that I hadn't explored before in this context, particularly with regard to the women in the Old Testament – so thanks for getting me to do that.

It has been helpful to think further about how I apply my understanding of male headship to my role as a woman in ministry. You challenged me (rightly) on taking the position I do, and yet teaching a mixed congregation. It might have saved me a bit of work if I had then come to the conclusion that I should only teach women!

As you struggle to see how I find hierarchy in Scripture with regard to leadership in the early church, I also struggle with how you understand Genesis, and there are many areas where we have had to agree to disagree. But it has particularly struck me in a deeper way than before that, while we may disagree over headship, it is so clear to both of us that women have equal worth and value. Women have an important part to play alongside men in furthering God's kingdom. So I hope this book does challenge people from whatever position they hold to think about how they can encourage women in their congregations to be involved in ministry.

We have both been through some tough times, as we have faced big changes and various bereavements. Through it all, I have appreciated your care and support. Although we differ on some things, it has been great that we are united on many others, especially in supporting women in ministry. Like you, I hope our discussions will encourage others to listen and talk together, to try to understand where others are coming from, and to give them credit for having grappled with the texts.

It has been a good experience, although at times it has been tough finding the time to write back. So often the arrival of an email from you coincided with a load of other deadlines – but what a great feeling it was to press the 'send' button and hand over to you! My family too will be very happy when the manuscript has been handed over to IVP. Who knows, maybe now when we meet up we can talk about other aspects of ministry, rather than headship and the role of women!

After all our discussion, I still remain firm on what I believe about male headship, but I have grown to understand the other side of the arguments more fully. There have been times when the conclusions have not been clear either way, and so there are challenges for both groups about how to apply what we believe Scripture teaches. If you were given an opportunity to address your constituency, what would you want to say?

I look forward to hearing back from you. I hope the various talks that you have planned for the coming week go well, and that you find the time for preparation. Tomorrow is the last of my teaching slots for this term at Wycliffe and Oak Hill – now there's just a sermon and a meditation to prepare. And after that, just the Christmas preparations – no problem!

Love in Christ
Clare

From:	**Lis Goddard**
To:	Clare Hendry
Subject:	Putting your money where your mouth is

Dear Clare

Thank you so much for your lovely email. As you say, we have been through a lot together, and this is what I was talking about when I referred to the relationship that God has given us. It has been wonderful to have someone walking alongside me, who I know has been praying for me and my family during some really tough times. Thank you for that, and for working at this with me. I really value so much the fact that you have been willing to walk this path with me in a way that some would not, that you have never doubted my integrity or the fact that I am struggling with Scripture just as you are. Thank you, Clare, for your friendship, which I am sure will last way beyond the publication of this book.

Has this experience left me with any reflections for those from my constituency? What a good question! Several things have particularly struck me throughout this process, things which are perhaps important for others.

First of all, there is the matter of process, the most basic thing that we have kept coming back to. I would want to challenge those in my constituency to be willing to engage with those from yours, to listen and to take the risk of working with them. There seems to be such a history of hurt and misunderstanding, and I keep coming across those who want to write off 'conservatives' without attempting to build relationships, often because they feel that they have already been written off first.

Second, I think that I am now even more convinced than I was before that single-sex leadership in a church is just not how it should be – whether that is all male or all female. Recently I decided not to apply for a job because all those in positions of leadership in that church were women. As you know, I do not think it matters who is in charge, as long as there is a balanced team, so I would want to say to my constituency, 'Don't make the same mistake you deplored the other way round.' Leadership should reflect the image of God, male and female, as in Genesis 1:28.

I would also want to say to my constituency, 'Put your money where your mouth is.' If you really believe that women should be in leadership, be sure to encourage and mentor your young, able female leaders just as much as your young men. Provide them with good female role models, and don't just work with the alpha male model of leadership – think outside the box! I can think of one large church that says it supports women's ordination and yet has never had a female curate, let alone an associate! Similarly, take 1 Timothy seriously and ensure that your women are just as well taught as your men; don't let a woman be criticized because she is poorly trained.

And finally, don't always give women the pastoral care jobs; some women want to do these and that is fine if it is their gifting. But, just as not all women are nurses, not all women are meant to be in charge of pastoral care: others will want to preach and teach, or get stuck in with evangelism! Let's really expect God to do great things with our women alongside our men – even as Jesus did!

I expect I could go on . . .

What would you want to say to your constituency, I wonder? Is there any overlap?

I have a meeting here tonight, so I am going to have to tidy up big time! Everything is in chaos, as this week I have had to give four talks, on top of everything else. This included an Advent carol service, which was great fun, but when we tried to process outside with our lighted candles as a witness to the future coming of Christ, we were stopped by a torrential downpour!

Looking forward to hearing from you again

With so much love as ever
Lis

From:	**Clare Hendry**
To:	Lis Goddard
Subject:	Hear! Hear!

Dear Lis

Thanks for getting back to me so quickly, especially since you have had so much to do in the last few days.

When I began to think about what I would like to say to my constituency, I was amazed at how much we do overlap, with the odd tweak here and there.

I agree with you that there is a history of hurt and misunderstanding with both of our groups. I think this applies to our dealings with other groups as well. In my **chapter** there is quite a mix of evangelicals and **Anglo-Catholics**, and one of the things I have really appreciated over the last few years is getting to know people from another **churchmanship**, and building bridges and developing friendships with them. So often our mistrust of others who hold a different theological position is based on ignorance. As Christians, we need to model respect for others, and show grace and humility as we seek to listen to and understand other people's views – which doesn't mean being 'wishy washy' in the position we take.

I was really interested to hear what you were saying about mixed leadership and how important it is to have balance. I must admit that I had not given any thought to the problems of female-only, single-sex leadership, but I think you make a good point. As you know, I think the ultimate leader in the local church should be a man, but I am very much with you in wanting a mixed leadership team. I do believe that God created man and woman to complement each other, which should be reflected in the way we run our churches.

Over the years there have been various debates on the subject of male headship. I remember one particular meeting, where the leaders of several large, conservative, evangelical churches met together to discuss the issue. I don't think we got much further than the basics, and there was little discussion of how male headship should be applied, what kind of things women can do or how they should be trained and supported in such work.

So my challenge to my constituency is like yours: 'Put your money where your mouth is.' For those who don't feel that women should be ordained at all, please make sure that the women who are working in your churches are trained well and given jobs where they can exercise their God-given gifts in an appropriate setting. I know of one church who helped to pay for a woman to be trained at theological college and then provided a job for her, working with women. If you have women volunteers in your church involved in teaching other women, how are you training them for this important task, and how much time are you investing in developing and equipping them? Sometimes it is difficult to find good, evangelical conservative women to speak at various events – not because there aren't gifted women out there, but because they haven't always had the opportunity of theological training.

For others who may be happy with women being ordained but only to the diaconate, where are the jobs? It may be tempting to appoint a male curate, as within a year he will be able to share the load of early communion services. But please have the courage of your convictions and be prepared to look at women curates who share your theological position on male headship, even if that means you do all the early communion slots.

We also need to provide opportunities for women with years of experience to be recognized and encouraged to continue to grow in ministry – so much harder where the normal paths of developing in leadership are not open to them because of their theological position. I love the job I am doing at the moment, but

I do wonder what the future may hold for me. When the time is right for a move, where do I go and what do I do?

You also talk about female role models. I say a loud 'Amen' to much of what you say here. We need to think more about the roles and models of leadership we provide, and to explore how we can nurture and develop both men and women as they work together in teams – not that all women (or men) operate in the same way. I certainly don't want to stereotype them in how they work or in the kind of work they do, be it pastoral care or teaching. But there are some general gender differences that are helpful to bear in mind, and team leaders need to be aware of them and treat people in a way that brings out their full potential. It's highly likely that men who are heading up a local church will have worked far more with men than with women, and may not have considered how to support women team members and develop their potential in ministry.

Well, the time is getting late, and I have a very early start tomorrow, so I must get this off to you. As I was writing this, I was thinking very much of situations within my Anglican setting. Much of what we have debated over the months (and years!), and even the challenges we have just voiced, are surely relevant to other denominations. I wonder what kind of conversations and experiences you have had with folk from other denominations.

Look forward to hearing back from you

Love
Clare

From:	**Lis Goddard**
To:	Clare Hendry
Subject:	They think it's all over . . .

Dear Clare
How very refreshing to discover that we agree on so much in the practical outworking. I am sure that how we live together is key,

and learning to honour one another and to recognize Christ in the other is vital to our witness in the world.

I think these questions are still live in most churches that are engaging with the Scriptures. A little while ago Andrew and I were invited to lead a day conference at a large Baptist church to speak on the subject of the family, and I got talking to the assistant pastor about this book. His response was to say how useful it would be, as this is a debate that keeps resurfacing. I recently attended a meeting on the subject of women's leadership, run by Willow Creek and hosted by a very large Elim Church in the centre of Bristol. This seemed to be a hot topic for quite a number of the churches represented there. So I think I can safely say that it's not just us!

This subject also continues to be of great interest among young people. I am on the Standing Committee of a Christian Union, and have been for some years now. I have found that successive groups of students come to us for advice on this matter. I think I have lost track of the number of times we have heard the debate rehearsed. This Christian Union hasn't had a woman president yet, and they have stopped inviting women speakers – so, as one of their standing committee, I cannot speak there! But I regard it as part of the work of supporting young Christians in ministry and helping them to discover what it means to live out the gospel among their friends; my own ministry comes second. I pray that they will learn something by that. If I am honest, I do not agree with them, and I will always tell them so if I am asked, but the decision is theirs and they invariably opt for the weaker brother principle (perhaps literally on both counts!). They take this to mean that they should adopt a more conservative line, rather than inter-preting it as caring for the women in their midst who are gifted and could lead or who need role models.

On another tack, a couple of weeks ago I was fascinated to discover Nell having a very animated MSN conversation (can you have an 'animated' MSN conversation?) with a friend who she went to Soul Survivor with about whether women can be called by God to lead, so it is clearly a hot topic among teenagers too!

Clare, thank you for being such a faithful correspondent – I have really enjoyed getting to know you better and sharing this experience with you. I am off now to get food on the table and to start thinking about the structure of our Christingle and Christmas carol services – what fun!

With so much love as ever in our Lord,
who came and who will return!
Lis

From:	**Clare Hendry**
To:	Lis Goddard
Subject:	. . . it is now

Dear Lis

I can't believe that I have just received your <u>final</u> email!

I have spent most of the day off work and in bed feeling yuk, but I wanted to get a reply to you today, so you have time to put everything together to send off to IVP.

Most of my friends who are ministers in other denominations are linked with the FIEC (**Fellowship of Independent Evangelical Churches**). They tend to be on the conservative side, and for many of them there is little debate in the leadership team, and full agreement over male headship. However, as one of them remarked, people come into their churches from other denominations, where women may have either led the church or at least played a major part in the leadership team. Others may have come to Christ within their church and now want to think about the role of women. Their only experience of leadership may have been in the secular world, and they want to see what the Bible has to say about it.

I was encouraged that the ministers I have been chatting with liked the idea of exploring both sides of the debate. They certainly did not want to brainwash any members of their congregation, but wanted them to examine the issues and see what Scripture has to say.

160 | THE GENDER AGENDA

In the last year or so, I have had conversations about the role of women in the church with a variety of women, some of whom are already involved in working in churches. One of them is a ministry assistant at St James's. She has been in various Anglican churches that take different positions on male headship, and now she wants to look at the subject for herself. I was thinking of showing her what we have written and using it as a basis to talk through the matter.

The debate over headship and the role of women in the church will continue in all the denominations. Our material wasn't available for the debate we had on this topic in our PCC, but I can see it being very useful in the future. When the time comes around again to appoint a new vicar, I imagine that most, if not all, the PCC members will have changed, and we will need to go back to see what Scripture says.

My prayer is that this book will be a valuable resource for others wanting to look at this whole area. I also hope it will encourage church leaders, both male and female, to think about how women (and men) can be encouraged to play their role in furthering God's kingdom as they use their gifts in his service.

Well, I hope you have a great Christmas and manage to enjoy some time with your family. I am certainly looking forward to that. My next task is to plan our last Thursday Focus (St James's Women's Fellowship). Knowing what an incredibly busy and manic time this is for women, I want to do something more meditative in the lead up to Christmas, to give us some space to think about the real significance of Christmas – the incarnation – and to forget, at least for a moment, all the gifts we still have to buy, cards to write, houses to decorate, food to prepare . . . and to concentrate on the greatest gift of all – God's Son.

With lots of love
See you in the New Year
Clare

To ponder

Reflect on what you have read in the last nine chapters.

- What have you learned?
- How has it changed and challenged you?
- How will it shape the way you live in relation to other Christians?
- Are there things about yourself you have learned? That you regret?
- How will you move on from here?

Pray

Thank God for brothers and sisters in Christ, that we are united in him, even when we disagree.

Thank God for his Word which constantly challenges and renews us by his Spirit.

Give yourself to God anew, and be committed to challenging those areas where things are not what they should be.

Glossary

Anglo-Catholics People, beliefs and practices within Anglicanism that affirm the Roman Catholic rather than the Protestant heritage of the Anglican Church.

Anthropology The study of humankind, including the comparative study of societies and cultures.

Apostles Literally means 'those who are sent'. Applied to various groups, most narrowly to the Twelve, more widely to witnesses of the resurrection, and most extensively to those who planted new churches.

AWESOME Anglican Women Evangelicals Supporting Our Ordained Ministries (http://www.awesome.org.uk). Lis and Clare both serve on the committee.

Babel Old Testament reference to when God's people built a tower to glorify man rather than God, and God consequently confused language so that people couldn't understand one another any more. See Genesis 11.

Chapter Regular gathering of Anglican clergy from the local area who meet for business, fellowship and prayer.

Charismatic A movement within evangelicalism, but also more widely in the church, which emphasizes the gifts of the Holy Spirit.

Churchmanship This term is sometimes used to refer to different understandings of church doctrine and liturgical practice which mark out distinctive groups within a denomination.

Commission The task God gave humankind in Genesis 1:26 to rule over creation.

Complementarity/complementarian A conservative view of the roles of men and women, encompassing male headship and male and female roles being complementary.

Concubines Women who live with a man but have a lower status than his wife/wives.

Conservative A group of evangelicals within the Church of England who have a high view of Scripture and tend to hold more traditional views on the role women within the local church.

Core constituencies Refers to the two evangelical groups that the authors identify with. The two groups differ mainly on what role women can take within the church (although even within the groups there is diversity).

Creation ordinance Order established by God at creation.

Curate Someone in their first training post in the Church of England; assistant to the vicar/rector.

CYFA Christian Youth Fellowship Association.

Deacon All ordained ministers in the Church of England remain deacons throughout their ministry, but some do not go on to be priested after their first year of ministry, but choose to remain a deacon. Used in the New Testament to describe both women and men set apart to serve God's people, freeing others to be presbyter (vicar/priest).

Deaconess A distinct office in some churches for women only, and similar to the office of deacon.

Diaconate The office of deacon.

Dionysiac A cult worshipping the god Dionysus.

Doctrine/Doctrinal Relating to Christian teaching.

Dog collar Nickname for the white plastic collar worn by ordained clergy.

Editors Those who brought together earlier biblical sources or arranged the original texts, in order to make them easier to read and to create the final biblical text.

Egalitarian An understanding of male/female roles which holds that men and women are equal.

Elder/Overseer One of the main leaders/teachers of a church.

Evangelical A tradition within Protestant Christianity which emphasizes the authority of the Bible, personal conversion and justification by grace.

Evangelists Those with a particular gift of sharing the gospel.

Extrapolating Inferring or conjecturing.

Fall, the When Adam and Eve rebelled against God in Genesis 3.

Fellowship of Independent Evangelical Churches (FIEC) An organization linking independent evangelical churches in the United Kingdom. Members share a common doctrinal basis.

Formula of counsel A technical term used for the words 'let us make' (Genesis 1:26), reflecting the personal nature/relationship between God and humankind.

Formula of fiat Fiat literally meaning 'let there be'. A technical term used for the words that God used when he created the world in Genesis 1.

Gnostics A group who believed that they had special knowledge of spiritual realities.

Gordian knot An intricate problem. According to Greek legend, it was a complicated knot tied by King Gordius, and cut through by Alexander the Great.

Hebrew The language in which the Old Testament was originally written.

Hermeneutic The theory and methodology of interpretation, especially of Scripture.

Judaizers Those in the New Testament church who required Gentile converts to accept Jewish law and customs, such as circumcision.

Kingdom of God/Kingdom, the The rule or reign of God which Jesus proclaimed and enacted, fully realized in the second coming.

Levitical priesthood/Priestly role of Levi In the Old Testament only men from the tribe of Levi were allowed to be priests within the Jewish faith.

Magnificat The hymn/song of Mary, mother of Jesus, responding to what God was doing through her (found in Luke 2:46–55).

Mariology The part of Christian theology concerned with the person and nature of the Virgin Mary.

Messianic mission The task of spreading the good news of the gospel.

Mosaic Law The Law that was given to the Israelite people through Moses and is contained in the first five books of the Old Testament.

Mutuality Total self-giving and interdependence between two people and in the Godhead.

Narrative The story spelt out in the chapters, normally distinctive from dialogue.

New creation/order The new world which God is establishing through the coming of Christ.

Normative An assumed norm; standard correct behaviour.

Old covenant The agreement that God made with his people in the Old Testament.

Ordination The ceremony where a person has holy orders conferred on them. See also **Deacon** and **Priesthood**

Pastoral office Someone who takes a leadership role in the church.

Pastors Those gifted and recognized as called to care for and nurture God's people.

Polygamy Practice of having more than one wife or husband at the same time.

Presbyter An elder or minister within the Christian church.

Priesthood/Presbyterate The ordained clergy in the Church of England, excluding those clergy who remain deacons; includes vicars and rectors.

Proof-text A Bible passage or verse that is used to make or prove a point, sometimes by taking it out of context.

Prophets Those who speak on behalf of God on the basis of hearing his voice or receiving a vision. Many see New Testament prophets as different from, and of lesser authority than, Old Testament prophets.

Redeemer, the Christ, the one who comes to redeem or save.

Relational subordination To advocate subordination based not on substance but on relationship.

Selection conference A three-day residential conference at the final stage of being selected for ordination training in the Church of England. Now called a Bishops' Advisory Panel.

Semantics Branch of linguistics concerned with meaning.

Septuagint Greek version of the Old Testament which was widely used at the time of the New Testament.

Sociology The study of the development, structure and functioning of human society.

Subordinationist The belief that God the Son is subordinate to God the Father. Also used in relation to those who believe women should be subordinate to men in marriage and church order.

Teachers Those gifted and recognized as called to teach God's people, whether through preaching or in other contexts.

Trinity The three persons of the Godhead: Father, Son and Holy Spirit. Also sometimes used as a synonym for God.

Triune Relating to the Trinity.

Words of Institution The words Jesus used to establish the Lord's Supper.

Further reading

General

Kenneth E. Bailey, 'Women in the New Testament: A Middle Eastern Cultural View' – a fascinating series of articles covering a whole range of NT issues surrounding women; originally published by Anvil, but now only available online at: http://www.cbeinternational.org/?q=content/women-new-testament-middle-eastern-cultural-view

Linda L. Belleville, Craig L. Blomberg, Craig S. Keener and Thomas R. Schreiner, *Two Views on Women in Ministry* (Zondervan, 2001). Helpful in getting to grips with some of the main arguments.

Catherine Clark Kroeger, Mary Evans and Elaine Storkey (eds), *Women's Study New Testament* (Marshall Pickering, 1995).

Kevin Giles, *The Trinity and Subordinationism: The Doctrine of God and the Contemporary Gender Debate* (Intervarsity Press, 2002).

Wayne Grudem, *Evangelical Feminism and Biblical Truth: An Analysis of 118 Disputed Questions* (Apollos, 2004), written from a complementarian viewpoint.

James B. Hurley, *Man and Woman in Biblical Perspective* (Wipf & Stock, 2002).

George W. Knight III, *Role Relationships of Men and Women: New Testament Teaching* (Presbyterian & Reformed, 1989).

Scot McKnight, *The Blue Parakeet: Rethinking How You Read the Bible* (Zondervan, 2008).

Werner Neuer, *Man and Woman in Christian Perspective* (trans. G. Wenham) (Crossway, 1991).

Philip B. Payne, *Man and Woman, One in Christ: An Exegetical and Theological Study of Paul's Letters* (Zondervan, 2009).

Andrew Perriman, *Speaking of Women: Interpreting Paul* (Apollos, 1998).

Ronald W. Pierce, Rebecca Merrill Groothuis and Gordon Fee (eds), *Discovering Biblical Equality: Complementarity Without Hierarchy* (Apollos, 2005).

John Piper and Wayne Grudem, *Recovering Biblical Manhood and Womanhood: A Response to Evangelical Feminism* (Crossway Books,1991).

Digging deeper

Kenneth E. Bailey, *Jesus Through Middle Eastern Eyes: Cultural Studies in the Gospels* (SPCK, 2008).

Richard Bauckham, *Gospel Women: Studies of the Named Women in the Gospels* (Eerdmans, 2002).

James Montgomery Boice and A. Skevington Wood, *Galatians and Ephesians*, The Expositor's Bible Commentary, Vol. 10 (Zondervan, 1996).

D. A. Carson, *Matthew*, The Expositor's Bible Commentary, Vol. 8 (Zondervan, 1984).

Richard Clark Kroeger and Catherine Clark Kroeger, *I Suffer Not a Woman: Rethinking 1 Timothy 2:11–15 in Light of Ancient Evidence* (Baker, 1998).

Gordon Fee, *The First Epistle to the Corinthians*, The New International Commentary on the New Testament (Eerdmanns, 1987).

Gordon Fee, *1 and 2 Timothy*, New International Biblical Commentary (Paternoster, 1995).

J. Harris, C. Brown and M. Moore, *Joshua, Judges, Ruth*, New International Biblical Commentary (Paternoster, 2003).

Morna D. Hooker, *From Adam to Christ* (Cambridge University Press, 1990).

Donald H. Madvig, Herbert M. Wolf and F. B. Huey Jr, *Deuteronomy, Joshua, Judges, Ruth, 1 & 2 Samuel*, The Expositor's Bible Commentary, Vol. 3 (Zondervan, 1992).

W. Harold Mare, *1 Corinthians*, The Expositor's Bible Commentary, Vol. 10 (Zondervan, 1976).

Scot McKnight, *The Real Mary: Why Evangelical Christians Can Embrace the Mother of Jesus* (SPCK, 2007).

Tim Perry, *Mary For Evangelicals: Toward an Understanding of the Mother of our Lord* (IVP Academic, 2006).

David Prior, *The Message of 1 Corinthians: Life in the Local Church*, The Bible Speaks Today (IVP, 1985).

John H. Sailhamer, *Genesis*, The Expositor's Bible Commentary, Vol. 2 (Zondervan, 1990).

A. Skevington Wood, *Ephesians*, The Expositor's Bible Commentary, Vol. 11 (Zondervan, 1978).

John Stott, *The Message of Ephesians*, The Bible Speaks Today (IVP, 1989).

John Stott, *The Message of 1 Timothy & Titus*, The Bible Speaks Today (IVP, 1996).

Anthony C. Thistelton, *The First Epistle to the Corinthians*, New International Greek Testament Commentary (Paternoster Press, 2000).

Ben Witherington III, *Grace in Galatia: A Commentary on Paul's Letter to the Galatians* (T. & T. Clark, 1998), see esp. pp. 261–281.

Tom Wright, *Paul for Everyone: Galatians and Thessalonians* (SPCK, 2002).

Tom Wright, *Paul for Everyone: The Pastoral Epistles: Titus and 1 and 2 Timothy* (SPCK, 2003).

Notes

Chapter 2

1. Werner Neuer, *Man and Woman in Christian Perspective*, trans. Gordon J. Wenham (Crossway, 1991), p. 72.

Chapter 4

1. See e.g. Kenneth E. Bailey, 'Women in the New Testament: A Middle Eastern Cultural View' (http://www. cbeinternational.org/?q=content/women-new-testament-middle-eastern-cultural-view), p. 2; and Scot McKnight, *The Real Mary: Why Evangelical Christians Can Embrace the Mother of Jesus* (SPCK, 2007). chs 3 and 4.

Chapter 5

1. Wayne Grudem, *Evangelical Feminism and Biblical Truth: An Analysis of 118 Disputed Questions* (Apollos, 2004), pp. 220–223.
2. R. C. Sproul, *The Gospel of God: Expositions of Paul's Letter to the Romans* (Christian Focus, 1999), pp. 249–250.

Chapter 6

1. Morna Hooker, *From Adam to Christ* (Cambridge University Press, 1990), pp. 113–120.
2. Wayne Grudem, 'The Meaning of *Kephalē*: An Evaluation of New Evidence, Real and Alleged' (Appendix 4) in Wayne Grudem, *Evangelical Feminism and Biblical Truth* (Apollos, 2004).

3. Anthony C. Thistelton, *The First Epistle to the Corinthians*, New International Greek Testament Commentary (Paternoster Press, 2000), pp. 812–814; Andrew Perriman, *Speaking of Women: Interpreting Paul* (Apollos, 1998), ch. 1.

4. Of the 2,336 instances of *kephalē* in ancient literature, 2,000 of them refer to the head (Anthony C. Thistelton, *The First Epistle to the Corinthians*, New International Greek Testament Commentary, Paternoster Press: 2000, p. 814).

5. Andrew Perriman, *Speaking of Women: Interpreting Paul* (Apollos, 1998), p. 33.

6. Linda L. Belleville, Craig L. Blomberg, Craig S. Keener, Thomas R. Schreiner, *Two Views on Women in Ministry* (Zondervan, 2001) pp. 155–156.

7. D. A. Carson, 'Silent in the Churches': On the Role of Women in 1 Corinthians 14:33b–36 in John Piper and Wayne Grudem (eds), *Recovering Biblical Manhood and Womanhood: A Response to Evangelical Feminism* (Crossway, 1991).

8. M. Hooker, *From Adam to Christ* (Cambridge University Press, 1990), p. 116.

9. Philip B. Payne, *Man and Woman, One in Christ: An Exegetical and Theological Study of Paul's Letters* (Zondervan, 2009), p. 195.

Chapter 7

1. James Hurley, *Man and Woman in Biblical Perspective* (Zondervan, 1981).

Chapter 8

1. John Stott, *1 Timothy and Titus* in The Bible Speaks Today series (IVP, 1996), pp. 74–81.

2. Philip B. Payne, *Man and Woman, One in Christ: An Exegetical and Theological Study of Paul's Letters* (Zondervan, 2009), p. 422.

3. Linda L. Belleville, Craig L. Blomberg, Craig S. Keener and Thomas R. Schreiner, *Two Views on Women in Ministry* (Zondervan: 2001), pp. 168–169.

4. Helen Campbell, 'One Woman's Way' in *The Briefing* (Issue 217, 1999).